PEANUT BUTTER AND PASSPORTS

DRIVING APES, SKIVVY SKYDIVERS AND TRAVEL TALES FROM AROUND THE WORLD

TOM GOSE

ISBN: 978-1-7320441-0-4

Disclaimer: This book describes the authors experiences while traveling and reflects his opinion of those experiences. Some names and details may have been changed to protect their privacy.

If you enjoy <u>Peanut Butter and Passports</u> please leave a review on Amazon.

DEDICATION

I love to see other people smile,
every day not once in a while.
Some people can annoy,
and take away your joy.
Ignore them, love your life in your style

Friends and family, you are loved.

To my four-legged posse
Sir William, Rosie, Ruby the Love Machine
and Tramp (the cat that we never called Tramp)
you're with me every day.

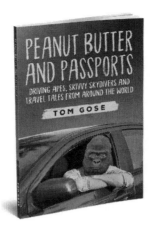

As my "Thank You" for buying
<u>Peanut Butter and Passports</u> I would love to
send you the FREE audio book version.

Please visit the URL below and I will send
you the audio book when it is produced.
https://tomgose.com/books/

Visit the authors website at TomGose.com.

Special discounts may be available
for bulk purchases.

Untucked Media LLC

If you would like to book Tom to speak at your event, contact him at Tom@TomGose.com

TESTIMONIALS OF TOM SPEAKING

Tom Gose refined all of the skills that make him a phenomenal motivational teacher. He is one of the best story tellers I have ever met, easily weaving an engaging, often hilarious narrative into a life lesson that can be put into practical use by the audience member.

Eric Cochran, Principal
Lindbergh High School

His ability to inspire athletes, employees, or graduates is very persuading for moving any group to achieve. He offers high-energy, with original humor . . . customized to any organization!"

Tom Bilyeu
Department Coordinator
Professor of Business

"A commonality of great coaches is their ability to communicate. An essential aspect of what makes a coach a fabulous communicator is a sense of humor.

Coach Gose's comedic timing has always been one of his biggest strengths as it allows strangers to feel as if they have known coach for decades."

Coach Ryan Banta
Author – The Sprinter's Compendium
MTCCCA Conference President

TABLE OF CONTENTS

INTRODUCTION   1

CHAPTER 1 – HAWAII   17

CHAPTER 2 – PERU   39

CHAPTER 3 – BOLIVIA   69

CHAPTER 4 – CUBA   91

CHAPTER 5 – CANADA   107

CHAPTER 6 – NEW ZEALAND   143

CHAPTER 7 – IRELAND   229

EPILOGUE   265

ACKNOWLEDGEMENTS   273

ABOUT THE AUTHOR   277

INTRODUCTION

Right now, there are tourists canoeing the Amazon River, hoping to spot an Anaconda while swatting at mosquitos the size of Blue Jays.

Meanwhile, in Las Vegas, a 25-year-old with a "Dad Bod" is waking up in a stranger's front yard, nudged by the foot of a cop.

People from all over the world are hiking the Inca Trail, burning too many calories to count, in order to add Machu Picchu to their list of conquests. They are super fit and make their entire weekly supply of healthy meals on Sunday.

Somewhere else two tourists are eating their fifth doughnuts for breakfast in a café they saw on the Food Network. His t-shirt is old enough to vote, and he plans to follow up the binge with a nap. They consider chubby to be charming, think climbing into a tour bus counts as a "good hike," and typically fight off last

1

night's hangover with goods from the bakery down the street.

They are all travelers, as are the countless versions somewhere in between, and I am one of them. I love to work out and eat healthy while being cursed with possibly the biggest sweet tooth known to mankind. I revel in the toughest hike or workout by knowing there will be pizza or assorted cookies soon to follow as a reward.

It is a very good thing that literally anyone is qualified to travel. Growing up in the suburbs of St. Louis, my parents were great, my sisters and I bugged each other daily, and my childhood was ideal.

I was never a boy scout and will always prefer a bed over a sleeping bag. My dad loved cars and could build or repair seemingly anything whereas I was only proficient at breaking things.

When I was about seven years old, my dad took me to a vacant lot that was used by kids on dirt bikes as a pseudo race track. With his encouragement, I hammered hard at the pedals, picking up speed in the hopes of making dad proud. Cruising off of a small mound caused a crash landing with the brunt of the impact being absorbed by my little 2nd grade marbles against the impressively unforgiving bike frame.

Sports involving wheels were out.

I loved sports, and cheered the local teams like young fans do. I was drawn to the training and intensity of wrestling and football and had some success in high school, which gave confidence to a kid who needed it.

I was good enough to receive a full-ride football scholarship to college yet bad enough for those coaches to regret it for five years. My football tenure at Southwest Missouri State University prepared me well for a career as a stuntman or crash-test dummy. I was over my head from a talent standpoint, and quitting sounded really good at first. However, giving up because it was hard wasn't my style, so I stuck it out.

My career statistics as a defensive tackle totaled: one fumble recovery, one tackle and multiple knee surgeries.

Graduating in 1991, I got hired to teach social studies at a high school in suburban St. Louis. The principal who hired me likely wasn't impressed by my 2.9 college G.P.A. or the fact it took three tries to pass college algebra. When he offered me the job, he said I would relate well to the students that didn't do well academically. As we shook hands I tried to figure out if that was a compliment or not. The world of teaching and coaching high school kids would dominate the next 25 years of my life.

I was passionate about teaching history. The discipline is nothing more than a story of people and events. When it is taught that way, it can be incredibly interesting. A major component of world history is the Era of Exploration. The men on these ships were brave beyond words and neck-deep in hardships.

If storms or pirates didn't do them in, getting lost just might. At times, the food supply was so low the crew had to eat rats from the ships' cargo hold. When the rat supply was exhausted they resorted to eating their shoes. It is a special kind of hunger that makes one eat their shoes.

These explorers were the men that made the maps for everyone else. They traveled the high seas in search of faraway lands and had no real idea where they were going.

Christopher Columbus, Ferdinand Magellan and the like, were absurdly tough men with supreme navigation skills. Many of their peers died on the expeditions due to bad luck or poor decisions. They had all of the skills and strength necessary to be successful but often were still beaten in the end.

I will travel anywhere at any time but will likely get lost getting out of my own neighborhood. I am definitely a man born in the proper century. Without modern navigation assistance, I would likely be the skeletal remains in an Under Armour hoodie found somewhere by hikers.

In the era *right* before high-tech, accurate navigation was built into cars and phones, I drove a rental box truck from St. Louis to Dallas to move my darling stepdaughter into her dorm. I happily drove the truck, while the ladies flew down ahead of me. A 10-hour drive became a 15-hour slog with me following my own directions.

Hitting detours in Tulsa, Oklahoma was the genesis of my miserable day behind the wheel. Afterward, I could have written an exhaustive guide book of every small town in the state as it felt like I passed through all of them.

In one old dusty town with a narrow Main Street, lined exclusively with "mom and pop" shops, I parked on the side of the road to fetch food and hopefully directions. Despite being a fit, normal-looking dude, I noticed people peering at me strangely as though I was "The Beast" of Disney fame.

This place was *w-a-y* off the main highway—a result of my fabulous navigating. It looked like each family reported to the local City Hall (which doubled as the barber shop) for their mandatory uniform of flannel and overalls.

The road looked like a used pickup truck sales lot. The only automotive innovation this town had seen was extended cabs. Walking out with trail mix and water, I realized this "wide-spot-in-the-road" town probably doesn't see many strangers in ball caps, Nike shirts and flip flops dropping by. I was in a neighboring state—and in a different world—all at the same time.

Late in the drive, I was tired, frustrated, and most of all, I was "Slap Happy." When surrounded with others feeling the same way, Slap Happy is hilarious. You laugh over things that really are not funny more because of fatigue than anything else.

In 2004, I was the head wrestling coach at the high school where I taught. The team was in Columbia, Missouri, for the State Championships, and this was the final day of a three-day trip that involved very little sleep, and big swings of emotion. Coaching athletes attaining success, or dealing with failure, at State is a grind. The *l-o-n-g* days take their toll.

The setting was ripe for "slap happiness" to set in.

As Josh, one of my coaches, and I drove through town with three athletes in the backseat, we talked about Josh's dog. It was the family dog he had grown up with, who was now very old and starting to struggle. You will not find someone more loyal to dogs and animal causes than me, so I was very empathetic to the situation.

It had gotten dark, which is never good for me. I can fall asleep at any time, and in any place. When darkness sets in, it is similar to dropping a cover over a parrot's cage. The bird thinks it is nighttime and stops making noise. Darkness has the same effect on me. That is helpful in many cases but definitely not while driving alone for 15 straight hours.

Despite being close to the campus, I needed coffee and walking around to stay awake. I pulled in to a convenience store and saw a guy walk out the front door. He was short and heavy—the kind of build that makes him as tall while laying down as he is standing. He dropped whatever he was carrying and bent down to pick it up.

As he stooped, reaching for the ground, his pants lost their battle with gravity and fell to his knees, revealing his own personal "Super Moon" to me.

I rarely laugh out loud, typically finding things merely amusing that others find hilarious. Still seated inside the uncomfortable box truck, I absolutely lost it. Swaying forward and backward, I was beating on the steering wheel and generally losing all composure.

The man realized what happened, quickly stood and snatched his pants up. He then bent down a second time to retrieve what he dropped only for the "Super Moon" to rise again.

At just that moment, a group of teenagers walked out of the store and saw him stooped over, mooning the world. They cackled uproariously with no attempt to hide it, which only fueled my laughter.

He swiped whatever it was off of the ground with one hand, while pulling his britches up with the other and waddled off quickly, tugging his pants up the entire way.

I continued to laugh convulsively in the cab of the truck for several minutes, doubtlessly looking like the tambourine-playing monkey. Coffee was no longer needed thanks to the adrenaline rush of laughing until I cried.

Good entertainment also comes when sitting in a stadium, on a park bench, in an airport terminal or any other public place and just watching who or what walks by. The pure comedy of watching other people in their state of normal is its own entertainment category.

People joke about falling down and getting up lightning quick as if it helps ensure that no one saw it. Like clicking the "undo" symbol on your computer. Other times, people do things and just hope they are invisible, while others are simply unconcerned with societal norms.

I once pulled up to a red light and the guy on my right had a finger in his nose. I'm talking knuckle deep. He glanced to his left, directly at me, as though he wasn't doing anything unusual. We shared an awkward glance directly at each other for five or six seconds. Perhaps he did not care, or he simply thought, "Nah . . ., he hasn't noticed." He was as nonchalant as if he *did not* have a finger jammed into his nose.

A Jedi mind trick of sorts that did not work.

In high school, I worked one summer at a local hardware store. It should have been an ideal gig, but I have *zero* aptitude for tools, hardware and the like. Customers would ask me where they could find lug nuts, and I would explain that we didn't sell food and suggest they try the nearest grocery store. It was more of a sketch comedy paying minimum wage than a summer job.

Arriving at work one day created a scenario where I was the unfortunate star of "people watchers."

My first car was a Ford Granada that my sister and I shared. Though it didn't look bad for that era, it had several "challenges." It would hack, sputter and die with great consistency and starting it was as easy as practicing gymnastics while wearing a body cast. It wasn't too long before the Granada had become a black and white photo on a mantle, having choked up its final hairball.

In its place was a Ford Escort. The Escort was a trooper, often hauling four or five people and loads of junk, it would cruise the highway at admirable speeds. Yes, the entire steering column shuddered intensely, but the trip was always completed. It was reliable but imperfect—like a packhorse with a limp.

It had other quirks too.

I arrived at the hardware store one afternoon and, after parking, I got out and walked away. The car was turned off, the keys were in my pocket and the doors were locked. Oddly, inexplicably, the windshield wipers were moving back and forth across the windshield.

Naturally, a stranger was getting out of her car near mine and noticed the rogue wipers doing battle with dirt. She said to me, "Hey, your wipers are on still." I kept walking and replied, "It's going to rain." wanting to distance myself from a car that did its best to embarrass me from time-to-time.

I am all in favor of high school and college kids driving cars a little past their prime. I think it's good—though incredibly undesirable at that age—to drive something that darn well may not start. It makes the game more interesting.

While in college, I had a nearly four-hour drive to make across the state of Missouri. The Escort was packed floor to ceiling, and it was best I didn't open the backdoors or hatchback until arriving home.

I hated long drives then, and this one would prove to be particularly brutal. Final exam times forced the drive into the evening on a day when the temperatures topped out around 20 degrees F (-7 C). By departure time, winds were whipping and temps were in single digits. The heater in the Escort wasn't working, and I underestimated how rough that would be.

An hour down the road, I was miserable. I could see my breath inside the car, my teeth chattered and full body shivering had descended upon me. I had to wear gloves to touch the steering wheel, and I was fairly certain my toes had frozen and snapped off inside my shoes.

There were three more hours to go.

Halfway home, in Rolla, Missouri, I stopped for gas. While it was pumping, I rummaged through what I could reach in the backseat without opening the backdoors. *Anything* that could provide warmth was welcome. I found a second pair of gloves and a Halloween style gorilla mask that you pull over your entire head. Lacking a hat, my ears were brutally cold, so the gorilla mask could only help.

I paid for the gas and hit the highway for the remaining two hours of the trip. In time, I adjusted to having no real peripheral vision. Traffic was sparse and my suffering was so intense that I truly forgot I was wearing the gorilla mask. I suppose the mask helped some, but the shivering was brutal. I was confident my ears were frostbitten too. I feared they would look like charcoal briquettes on the side of my head.

Arriving in the outer reaches of St. Louis county gave me hope. It felt like I was home, but in reality, there were still over 30 minutes to go. Just *getting home* sounded better than winning a lottery. Being in the suburban area of a metropolis, traffic volume had certainly increased. Darkness and hypothermia kept me focused on the road and blind to the fact I was wearing the gorilla mask. Drivers around me weren't so oblivious.

As I pulled off the highway, just five minutes from home, I sat at a red light. A car rolled up alongside, on my left. Extraordinarily eager to just get home, I looked about impatiently, waiting for the red to turn green. Looking left, the driver beside me was just staring at me. Nothing else. No smile or obscene gesture, but simply an intense glare.

Was he a "gear head" looking for a drag race? What kind of a jerk challenges a compact car stuffed with junk to a drag race? Maybe he was just a societal turd looking for a fight? Or maybe a guy who always looks like his worst possible mug shot?

Not knowing his deal, I looked forward as the light turned green. I started accelerating and the man on my left honked. Looking over, he gave me a "thumbs up" and with the passenger window down yelled, "Nice mask!"

I am not sure if he survived the blast of cold air, but only then did I realize countless others had likely glanced over to see the head of an ape behind the wheel. Though I had forgotten I looked like an escapee from a zoo, I certainly wasn't invisible like the nose-picking driver apparently thought he was.

I lack many traditional "man skills." My tool box is full of duct tape, I hate yard work, don't know one type of craft beer from another, have no real sense of direction and I like sappy Christmas movies.

Luckily for me, I have an abundance of the talents needed for adventuring about the world: people-watching skills and the ability to laugh at life's absurdities. The rest of this book will take you through my travels thus far in life, along with my observations of people along the way.

I would wish I was invisible a few years later in Honolulu, when once again, strangers couldn't help but notice something wasn't right.

CHAPTER 1 - HAWAII

My first trip to an island was in 1995, at age 27. My family made a trip to Hawaii over the Christmas holiday break. The trip was going to be long, running the entire length of my time off from teaching. The days leading up to it were hectic, trying to get final exams graded and other end-of-semester things done.

In the planning and packing whirlwind, I was in a rush to get to the airport. Having more things to do, than time to do them, is never good. Last minute errands to the post office and Blockbuster video did not go smoothly.

Many of us look back on the memories of browsing the aisles at Blockbuster in search of the perfect movie. The Horror aisle, then the Drama aisle. Row after row of genres. The frustration when *every* copy of a hot movie was taken. The aggravation of fines built up by failure to return videos on time. Fighting, or caving into, the temptation to buy theater candy which taunted us near the register. Movie shopping wasn't a perfect experience, but I admittedly browsed those stores in no rush, as I do book stores.

Now that same search takes place from home. Shopping from one's arse means no impulsive buying of licorice, Dots or Jujyfruits. I am not sure if that's a good or bad thing. There is no concern for the movie being sold out either, *and* you don't have to return it. It cannot get easier. Rest in Peace Blockbuster—you made a lot of people happy.

In a hurry, I raced through a post office mail drop and then headed to Blockbuster. As I walked up to the Blockbuster return slot, I realized there was a problem. Having just left the post office, why did I still have mail in my hand?

Nooooooo! I had dropped the videos in the mailbox.

I definitely did not have time for that.

Having returned to the post office, I explained my error much to the delight of several federal employees. They laughed and said it was no problem at all. Highly embarrassed, I was glad to know this was not the first time someone had dropped videos in their mailbox. They sent me on my way and actually returned the videos for me, as I left a vapor trail to the airport.

Packing for beaches should be easy. I had never packed for a trip over a week in length and packed for every possibility. I arrived at the airport carrying enough duffel bags and suitcases for five people. It would have been fitting to have walked up to the gate with two pack mules in tow. At family gatherings, this is still laughed at. Naturally, I only used about half of what I brought.

We arrived to all of the splendor that is Hawaii. Just days before Christmas, it was strange walking around in shorts and flip-flops. Honolulu decorates for Christmas just like all cities. Christmas trappings just look different on tropical islands.

To a guy from the Midwest, palm trees have a Pavlovian effect. They make any place look better. I was recently in Las Vegas. Though it was my fourth time visiting, I had forgotten that short mountains are everywhere you look and palm trees line the streets. The parts of the city I visited had a resort-like vibe for that reason. Even Walmart had a sparkle—something rarely said of a Walmart—because of the palm trees out front. On sight, palm trees make you feel like you're in a special place when you come from fly over country. Hawaii is definitely a special place.

As we move through life, there are always certain mental images that remain locked in place. Things you can visualize from the past when something triggers the memory. It may be of a strange facial expression, a friend laughing, a stranger stumbling and flailing about trying to regain their balance or the instant someone leaps out from hiding to scare the mess out of another person. What you remember can vary but things always stand out.

Naturally, it is always better to be the one *seeing* the memorable reaction than to be the star of that show. In time, all of us are familiar with both sides of that situation. On our trip to Hawaii, my brother-in-law, Fred, and I were on the wrong side of embarrassment on more than one occasion.

Early in our stay, a couple of guys in our group, including Fred, rented mopeds. Fred was a power lifter, the type of guy that could punch a building to death. He has a great sense of humor and was a fun travel mate. Driving through Honolulu, I was in a car in front of them. I looked back at a hilarious sight.

Six-foot tall and thick, Fred looked like a Brahma Bull sitting on a mushroom. Right behind him, a huge bus loomed dangerously. He dwarfed the moped and the bus dwarfed him.

I am sure the moped would have preferred a gymnast as a passenger as it strained to move at a pace appropriate for "main drag speed." The bus lurked ominously behind them. The guys avoided bad luck despite travelling at lawn mower speeds on a main road. I am sure drivers behind them don't remember it so fondly. This *is* America after all—the home of road rage.

A couple of nights later our group went to Planet Hollywood for dinner. We sat around, having a great time, and talked for a while after devouring a lot of food. On the way back to our hotel, I was stricken with a sudden emergency-level need to find a bathroom.

We still had over a mile to go on our walk. I didn't feel sick, but this was *urgent,* and everyone seeing me *had* to know because, in situations like this, one starts walking funny.

As things become more and more urgent, your gait changes. There seems to be more bending the knees and smaller, quicker steps. Occasionally there is a sudden full-body twitch, like a seizure, lasting half a second.

All of this was occurring while I was trying to be as discreet as possible, which likely only made the pace slower and the situation worse.

The struggle to the hotel bathroom was now a crisis situation.

As I got closer, there was no chance—*no* chance—that people didn't notice my issue. Walking hurriedly, knee's pinched together as though wearing a tight, knee-length skirt, I hoped for invisibility but knew better. By the time I entered the hotel lobby there was only one hope of avoiding a legendarily embarrassing situation.

The lobby bathroom—if there was one.

Little kids are famous for the "pee pee dance." It is kind of cute and charming when a five-year-old does it. At 27, it has no redeeming quality. Poor decisions were made along the way. There were places I could've stopped. This intestinal thunderstorm was capable of turning into an F5 tornado. Knowing that pushed me past those places in the hopes of getting to my private bathroom.

This contorted walk/shuffle picked up speed as I glanced for a restroom sign. Seeing it, I turned left—all the while praying. By the grace of God, it wasn't occupied, but strangely, the stall door was closed.

Opening the latch—so simple a thing an ordinary chimp could figure it out—was incredibly complicated due to the full body movement needed to buy myself time. One hand was unbuckling the belt and unzipping the fly while the rest of me spasmed like an alien war dance. I am not sure, from a biological view, why such strange jittering helps slow the inevitable tsunami. Maybe it doesn't; it just gives the brain something to focus on while your last seconds of dignity expire. Or possibly it's a form of the Placebo Effect, which though 100% mental, is still an effect.

Fortunately, the "open the latch, drop the shorts, *aaaaahhhhhh*" timing was as flawless as that of an Olympic gymnast on the pommel horse.

I was spared being the dude chronicled in "Do you remember that guy in Hawaii . . ." stories told around the world for decades. I would have embarrassed every twig and branch on the family tree.

Business was resolved amazingly quickly. The only good part of a looming bowel catastrophe is the enormous satisfaction of it being resolved without incident. Just like after a sickness, merely feeling normal again is appreciated.

Realizing I had slinked through the lobby with an obvious problem, I didn't return there. I found a side staircase to climb, hoping everyone in the lobby would never see me again.

At the beach one day, some of us were in the water. I was out pretty far—well beyond standing depth—enjoying the rise and fall of the waves. The invincibility of youth has its merits. At that age, I never worried about what may be lurking below.

Well into middle age now, I would still go scuba diving with no hesitation. The shift lies in having *no* interest in floating or swimming on the surface, not knowing what may be below. At least underwater, you can see what may be looking at you.

If you bring up the topic of sharks stalking and preparing to ambush you, surfers and water lovers wave you off as though you're silly and deny any concern. *"What are the odds it will be me?"* they think, overlooking the likelihood the last victim of a shark thought the very same thing.

Transfer that attitude to other places and this scenario would sound incredibly shady. People would never agree to being secretly watched and then possibly attacked.

If, for example, I offered a spare bedroom to a traveler, but told them their every move may be watched and it may involve them being ambushed and attacked, they would scream, run to their cars and call the police.

Imagine being in a movie theater. As the lights dim, you lean forward to the people in front of you and whisper, *"This may not happen—there are plenty of OTHER people in the theater I could do this to—but I may just sit here staring at you, waiting for the perfect moment to attack."* There would be bedlam as you are battered by their popcorn container, pelted with theater candy, and then pepper sprayed and beaten when the cops arrive.

Yet, people hang out in the ocean knowingly being watched by things they cannot see that could hurt, kill or even *eat* them, and seemingly have no concern at all.

People are strange like that.

Later, we were in shallower water throwing a Nerf football—typical stuff. Eventually, I walked toward the beach, kind of lost in thought. The setting so incredible, I trudged forward obliviously. Still about waist deep, I headed right toward my family who waved to get my attention on the crowded beach.

Waves crash here regularly. I had been in the water for a couple of hours and should have been more aware. Bearing down on me from behind was a huge wave. I will assume it was huge—I can't say that I saw it. One instant I was walking with sunglasses perched on my head, the next I was blindsided by an angry wave. If you have ever seen a football quarterback get drilled from behind you have an idea what this looked like.

My face was literally planted into the sand under the water. Stunned by the power of the wave, I pulled my head out of the ostrich position and staggered to my feet.

My family is one that enjoys laughing at itself so finding them was easy. They were the ones laughing hysterically. It occurred to me later that not only did they laugh at my destruction, they saw it coming from behind. There was no attempt to warn me. They just sat back and enjoyed the show.

In fairness to them, I should not have needed a warning. Being in the ocean and oblivious of waves is stupid, to be kind.

A short time later, I was buying new sunglasses. The ones perched on my head before getting jackhammered were missing. Perhaps they're on the ocean floor beside some shipwreck, floating to Tahiti or were swallowed by a whale.

Thankfully, there was no YouTube then. Nor smart phones. I can see the title on the video—"Dude gets destroyed by a wave!"

We ended the trip with a few days on the island of Maui, which may be the best tropical environment the U.S. has to offer. It was much less densely populated and commercialized than Honolulu.

One day, three of us decided to golf. We expected the greens fees to be outrageous, and there *were* courses that could cause sticker shock, but we found one we could play for only $30.

It was about a 45-minute drive, and being a cheap municipal course, we didn't expect much in the way of quality. We were stunningly wrong. The course had many holes right on the ocean with others bordering mountains.

I have played Torrey Pines, the famous course near San Diego. It has some stunning ocean view holes, and a world-class reputation, but is not nicer than this course. It was an incredible value for the cost.

Capable of hitting magnificent golf shots, all three of us are much more likely to play an entire round without hitting a single one. Some of my best forest hikes have been while looking for my golf ball. We fall deeply into the category of "golfing hacks."

My best round ever was 79. Playing the same course the very next day, I shot 99. Consistently inconsistent. We may not be good at golf, but we played fast and had fun with the best of them.

One memorable shot, which epitomized our ineptitude. Fred, the power lifter that rode the moped, stood over a tee shot and swung mightily. Capable of crushing a golf ball, he could easily send it well beyond the big boy mark of 300 yards.

His swing finished high into a pose looking far down the fairway. The ball went, generously, 15 feet.

He hit maybe the top dimple on the ball. It is hard not to laugh when a tee shot goes the distance of a free throw, so we laughed. True to the etiquette of the game, Fred got in the cart for the 15-foot drive.

We played awfully but had a great time. The cheapest course on the island was incredibly beautiful.

One day our group took a boat ride with about 50 others out to the Molokini Reef which is a few miles off the coast of Maui. We planned to go snorkeling and looked forward to it. On the ride out, one of the crew members announced that they had scuba gear available if anyone was interested in doing that instead of snorkeling.

I was immediately intrigued but didn't have scuba certification, which I believed was mandatory. I asked if we needed to be certified and the guide said, "No, we'll teach you everything you need to know." I loved that answer, but it was dubious at the same time. Most scuba, technically S.C.U.B.A (Self Contained Underwater Breathing Apparatus) certifications require nearly ten training dives and 20-30 hours of time invested into them.

So, despite being happy I could do it, being "trained" in about 30 minutes just might gloss over some important things. Not to worry, if something comes up, I can always ask a question underwater, right?

About ten people signed up. We were given a crash course in scuba lingo and taught the hand signals that constitute speaking underwater, one of which was the classic "thumbs up," which simply means "everything is okay." There were others hand signs too, but I forgot them immediately.

Upon arrival, the boat dropped anchor. Crew members divided themselves between the larger group of snorkelers and the scuba divers. The scuba crew entered the water one at a time and were told to hold onto a small rope attached to a bigger rope connected to the anchor.

Each of us held our own small rope and dangled near the surface as the rest of the scuba divers jumped in. I was the first in the water and wound up farthest from the boat to allow space for the others. I was just a few feet under the surface, waiting for the group, wondering why we had to all descend together.

I had expected some kind of scuba diving version of elementary school recess where each of us darted about doing our own thing. Thinking about it, I realized that keeping the crew together was really smart since we had essentially gotten "infomercial" level training.

The downside of ten people hanging in a cluster would be the arrival of a hungry Great White Shark who could bite off multiple people's limbs all in one drive-by attack. That possibility passed quickly because we wouldn't be together for long.

Suddenly, the rope I was holding broke free from the anchor line, and I began to drop. I was briefly glad it was time to swim until I realized I was the *only one* dropping. Looking up, I could see the rest of the crew still near the surface.

As I descended, I quickly felt like my head was in a vice getting squeezed. As I continued to fall, the pressure-like discomfort was replaced by a worse pain. It felt like a woodpecker with a dagger for a beak was having its way with my head.

At this point, one of the scuba passengers noticed me plummeting and urgently grabbed the guide, while pointing down at me. I have taken hundreds of "other people's kids" on overnight trips to compete in one sport or another as a high school head coach. Though I wasn't a kid in this scenario, I am pretty sure I knew what the guide was thinking, and it wasn't "Rated G."

He dove toward me with impressive speed while I had a flash of common sense, realized I didn't have to keep dropping and began treading water. I was likely 30 meters deep when he arrived.

Certified scuba divers are trained to "equalize," or manage, the pressure in their ears every five or so feet during a descent. Just like when landing in an airplane, pinching the nose shut and blowing against it creates a pain-relieving "pop" in the head.

The pain in my head should have reminded me of that, but I was distracted by the woodpecker. The guide arrived beside me shockingly quickly and formed a circle with his index finger and thumb with the other digits standing tall to ask, "Are you Okay?"

We were taught a sign for this, but that had long been forgotten. I substituted pointing at my head repeatedly with both index fingers. My eyes likely bulged as though I had been donkey-kicked in my dangling participle.

He immediately motioned for me to pinch my nose and equalize. Doing so immediately brought on a "pow" internally that I thought may have sent a tsunami in some direction. The relief was incredible. He looked at me intently, either checking for blood from my ears or wondering if my IQ exceeded my shoe size.

We swam up, then came back down with the entire crew. We had been told to stay within sight of him when the free swim time came. Perhaps not surprisingly, he stayed very close to me the rest of the hour we spent on, or near, the floor of the Pacific Ocean.

I cannot recommend scuba diving highly enough. The types and colors of fish I saw seemed truly cartoonish. Someone highly skilled in animation would be lucky to do this well. We all have a few moments in life that we never forget. For me, this was one of them. I made note of it, saying to myself, "*You are standing on the floor of the Pacific Ocean,*" while there taking it in.

At one point, a bright orange fish with white stripes swam from my right to left. As it did, it turned and faced me. I am not sure if he could see me or not since fish eyes don't always face forward. The fish and I had a staring contest for five or six seconds before the tall, thin fish turned and carried on its way. It was remarkable seeing the assortment of fish. Our maximum depth of that dive was sixty feet (about 18 meters), and it made me realize that the depths of the oceans are almost like an entirely different world.

As is typically the case, the hour flew by and we were back aboard the ship cruising toward Maui. The scuba crew high-fived and reveled in the moment. The guide sat beside me to ask, "What do you think?" Stumbling over ten superlatives, I finally mustered, "I was surprised there weren't any sharks?"

He replied, "Oh, there were sharks, I just didn't point them out to you. It's sometimes best for rookies to not know."

After the woodpecker attack, nothing would have phased me.

Later in the trip, New Year's Eve approached. A few of us attended a concert at the Hard Rock Café. A band— The Rembrandts—was playing. The Rembrandts had a hit song at the time—the theme for the crazily popular TV sitcom "Friends."

We were excited about the opportunity. Hawaii is a very unique place to spend New Year's Eve. A small-venue concert in Hawaii makes for an even more unique night.

Anyone who has reached their 30s or older has lived long enough to have a certain perspective on life.

The older you get, the greater the perspective. As people age, their sense of fun changes considerably. When I was in high school and college, there was not a weekend night where I wouldn't go out in search of shenanigans.

Most people are active and party in college. When they first start their career, happy hours and "going out" on weekends is still the plan. For a few years after college, long weekends, road trips and all sorts of fun rule the day.

Then "it'" happens. You reach the stage where, around noon on Friday, the most glorious sounding thing is your couch.

By my 30s, I was deep into a career. The daily teaching and coaching combination was a grind. Work weeks would typically total 60 or more hours. For most of my career, I coached three sports each school year. Those absurdly long weeks would get stacked on top of each other.

Teachers tend to believe there is no kind of tired like "teacher tired" on Friday night. That may well be true. People in the workforce with similar hours know what it feels like at week's end. At my peak "grind stage," my life consisted of "Teach, Coach, Couch."

Transitioning from truly young and active to the more sedentary adult life is tough. Dreaming of your couch but having already made plans to go out is stage one.

This is particularly awful on a cold winter night when that glorious couch is all the more attractive. A sofa with a blanket, a fireplace, a favorite drink, your special someone, and a show to binge on is all the excitement you can handle.

As you layer up to deal with the cold, there is regret. You drive through fatigue that makes you feel drunk, and plan an exit before you get there. Arriving with a fake perkiness, you enjoy an hour or two before the exit strategy is deployed.

On this trip, at 27, I realized my priorities were changing. We sat inside the Hard Rock Café with The Rembrandts—an environment that is hard to beat on New Year's Eve. About 10 PM, I started getting tired. A few short years before that, I was just *leaving* to go out at 10 PM.

The music was great and most of the crowd was totally into it. To me, however, watching the time became more interesting than the band. By 11 o'clock, nothing sounded better than just going home. If my group wanted to stay, how could I leave without appearing boring? When you're young, the dreaded boring tag is like leprosy. I could have faked a seizure and caught some sleep on the way to the hospital but It seemed a touch extreme and likely illegal.

During that transition phase, no one wants to be the first person to bring up, "Hey, does anyone else want to leave?" Fortunately for all involved, someone eventually does. Standing 25 feet from the stage, I was that guy on New Year's Eve in 1995.

We were home by 11:30.

You would think that we would be rested enough on vacation to not feel that same "tired." The vast majority of travelers will admit they need a vacation after their vacation.

Traveling is phenomenal, but it is not restful.

Departure day arrived. The fabulous Hawaii vacation would now be a great memory.

The flight time to St. Louis was about eight hours. At that time in my life, eight hours seemed awful. Having since traveled to New Zealand, eight hours is easier than kindergarten math.

We had stretched the trip in length as long as possible. We were scheduled to arrive in St. Louis in the middle of the evening, and I had to teach the next morning.

I had not yet traveled far enough east to experience jetlag, though I had certainly heard of it. To deal with the eight-hour flight in an era before smart phones, laptops or tablets, I took some over-the-counter sleep aids.

Best idea ever.

I absolutely may have been the guy everyone laughed at—maybe sleeping with the head back, mouth open and maybe drooling. I was nudged awake about 20 minutes before landing. Still groggy, I heard the pilot tell the passengers that St. Louis had received a lot of snow.

Realizing the possibility, I threw the full force of hope and positivity towards the idea that we would not have school the next day. A "snow day" immediately after a great vacation would be an amazing gift.

Arriving home later, I hurriedly unpacked and tried to get settled so the next day would have some normalcy to it. Then the phone rang.

In the pre-internet days, teachers spread snow day joyousness through a phone chain. A friend from work delivered the news—*no school*!

I think he had been drinking.

I imagine there can be no more adrenalized feeling than matching the numbers on your lottery ticket to the winning digits. As the first two match, the drama builds, reaching a crescendo as you read each number and realize you've won. Then the "freak out" happens.

I would prefer winning an actual lotto, but this snow day was a small version of one. Even better, we missed the day after that as well. I have always been a believer in serendipity. Getting two snow days following an epic, exhausting trip was as serendipitous as life can get.

Anyone who gets to visit Hawaii is pretty lucky. More people dream about it than actually get to do it. Despite some really strange and unfortunate minor things that have happened to me over the years, by and large I have been very lucky.

I would learn a lot about luck of all types on my next trip to Peru.

CHAPTER 2 - PERU

In 2004, my co-worker Clint and I were talking about traveling. He had been a lot of places internationally while I had only traveled domestically. We hatched a plan for a trip to Peru and Bolivia. Machu Picchu was the main focus, but there were other things planned as well.

Traveling with Clint is fascinating. He is a generation older and has literally been to each continent and too many countries to track. This was my first international trip, so his experience made things easier. He is incredibly intelligent despite hiring me to teach in his high school's history department.

I wrangled a passport and packed. I had a nice camera, with a zoom lens and enough film for a Hollywood wedding. A digital camera, fairly new in 2004, certainly would have been more convenient. It is odd to think that using the camera in your phone wasn't even possible yet. Facebook was brand new then. Twitter and Instagram didn't even exist.

In the shower at 3:30am, I was at the start of a *l-o-n-g* day of travel. Who knew that toweling off one's head carried risk. While drying my dome, I was racked with back spasms—the crippling type if you have had them. Stepping out of the tub/shower combo was a challenge. Any unpredictable movement, like slipping, stumbling or getting bumped brought hellish pain.

I arrived at the airport with two suitcases and a *distinct* lean forward and to my right. The Tower of Pisa looked vertical compared to me. Clint, upon seeing me, asked, *"What happened to you?"* and I explained the dangers of drying off after a shower. Making the trip would be difficult, but staying back was never considered.

It was just pain, right?

I recently heard of a story from a radio show. As retold by the afflicted, he once sneezed so hard, *while on the toilet*, that he gave himself crippling back spasms and fell off the commode. His wife had to come and rescue him. That's true love (or an imminent divorce).

I have had back spasms a lot in life and they are pure misery, but there is *absolutely no chance* I'd cry for help after sneezing myself off of the toilet.

As nutty as it sounds that someone can be left in stabbing pain from drying off with a towel, I have had numerous strange things happen to me in the course of daily life. On the trip to Hawaii, I was the victim of a bird bomb across my right shoulder and head. The evidence suggested the bird who got me was the size of a pterodactyl.

More recently, I sat in a restaurant booth across from my parents. When the waitress brought my dad's potato soup she accidentally set the bowl down, overlapping the very edge of the table. Taking her hand away from it, she realized the problem, and instinctively, tried to catch the falling bowl. In doing so, she flipped the bowl into the air with 90% of the thick soup landing on my head. No one else at the table had a drop on them.

The crash of the bowl landing, along with the gasps of the waitress, drew a hush over the restaurant. The waitress stepped back covering her face, horrified at what happened. Other patrons and employees, even from the kitchen, were moving to get a better glimpse of the aftermath.

I sat motionless with soup dripping from my head.

I took it in stride realizing she was terrified of my reaction and maybe losing her job. I encouraged her and the other people to go ahead and laugh. It *was* hilarious. The manager asked if he could get me anything. I answered, "A towel?" apparently forgetting the dangers that towels represent. A couple of young employees giggled like hyenas behind me as I walked to the restroom, towel in hand.

Suffering back spasms the day of a long international flight is definitely bad luck. The spasms leaving me stooped over promised to make the long day of travel miserable.

The agenda? A flight from St. Louis to Miami, a six-hour layover, then over six more hours flying to Lima, Peru. Getting into or out of an airplane seat in such condition was no easy thing. Unfortunately, there was a lot of moving about. The lady beside me on the first leg of the trip visited the bathroom with unwelcomed frequency. She may not have had a bladder.

The ups and downs of turbulence were another painful plot twist. Each dip caused mumbled cussing and strange facial expressions. My fingers may have left impressions on the arm rests. My seatmate with the bathroom fetish seemed to not notice—her head-phones and mask hiding her from my suffering. It's possible, though, the "bathroom trips" were actually visits to the pilot to explain she was seated next to a grunting, crazed-looking lunatic.

Upon arriving in Miami, the six-hour layover was savored. I was the guy stretched out on the floor near the gate. Lying flat on my back provided relief. Getting up from the floor to board the plane was awful. The muttering, moaning and grimacing scared a young boy next to me, who hid behind his dad's legs while looking at me like I was a gargoyle.

Not my most impressive day.

I had no preconceived mental picture of Lima. I knew Peru, a developing country, would lack in many ways compared to our norm. We de-boarded the plane onto the Tarmac—not uncommon outside the U.S. Lima had beautiful palm trees and all of the vistas that coastal cities can provide. The oddity I noticed was how disparate one building would be compared to the one immediately next to it.

In the U.S., and in most of the developed world, entire neighborhoods have a common look. Many are neat and tidy, though the occasional odd, reclusive neighbor stands out either due to his civil war mutton chops, the front yard resembling wild Africa or the assortment of 50 pets.

Maybe all of the above.

Urban legends about that family and house are plentiful, but they are the lone suspected loon for blocks. Generally, things are familiar for vast areas.

Nearby, there may be an entirely different neighbor-hood that is, well—a 'hood. Another may have McMansions wedged onto small lots like elephants sitting on stools. Those designs and financial situations are located among others similar to them.

Downtown Lima in 2004, had wealth intermingled with ramshackle poverty. Shiny, gleaming, modern skyscrapers sandwiched between buildings covered in graffiti. The ragged buildings were in such rough shape it didn't look like they could survive the weight of an alley cat climbing the stairs. More of the city was poor than wealthy, though the international embassies added authority to some nicer neighborhoods.

Our first evening after arriving was destined to be a fantastic meal. Hunger and I being conjoined twins, I looked forward to dinner. Peru is a coastal country and, with Lima perched on the Pacific Ocean, seafood would be excellent. There was a local delicacy that, in the U.S., we call Guinea Pig. Peruvians call it Cuy (pronounced "Qwee"). I knew of Cuy before arriving but couldn't pull the trigger on trying it. Even though I didn't grow up with guinea pigs, I consider them pets. Eating one would be like devouring a horse burger. It's not going to happen.

We were seated in a very nice restaurant looking over menus when I saw a waiter carry a large platter of entrées past me. Glancing to my right as he passed, I noticed something very—unusual. Seconds later, so did the person that ordered it.

The guinea pig appeared to be cooked with the fur still on it. Guinea pigs can also be prepared like a pig roast on a rotisserie spit. When cooked that way, the guinea pig looks a lot more like a dead animal than a meal. Perhaps, the Cuy merely showed up looking like a dead, naked guinea pig. In either case she didn't expect it.

Screams in restaurants are rare—even getting hot soup dumped on my head didn't cause one. Her shriek was noticeable. I am sure drinks were spilled and forks were dropped around the restaurant. Maybe a Heimlich maneuver, or two, were needed.

The apologetic waiter scurried away with the pig, hoping to bring her something less "animal" looking, like broccoli. A couple of minutes of awkwardness dissipated as the chatter and clatter of restaurant ambience returned to normal. I cannot swear the lady's appetite ever did.

Two days later, with my back at about 80%, we went on a guided group tour of some ancient Incan ruins.

This required some hiking and bouldering which typically would be light work. At one place, the guide explained we would have to move through a tunnel. It's ceiling was so low that getting through it required army crawling on your chest and stomach while pushing your backpack ahead of you.

At the other end of the tunnel was a small landing with a view of a staggeringly-deep valley. The first few in our group began the crawl, disappearing from sight. I *knew* that a flare-up of the back spasms could leave me stuck inside the tunnel. Realizing that wasn't the best idea for me, I spotted a trail that appeared to go around the tunnel. Taking the trail seemed more appealing than CNN camera's documenting me in full gargoyle-mode being rescued. I told Clint and took the trail. It didn't occur to me to mention it to the guide.

I should have.

For the first 30-40 steps on the trail, the detour appeared to be a good decision. The final several dozen steps proved otherwise. The trail circumvented the tunnel while ascending up toward the aforementioned landing. With each step, I started to wonder if this *was* a trail. It got narrower, and narrower.

Eventually, it was an eight or nine-inch lip that required me facing the sheer rock face. Progress was now scooting sideways while clutching the cliff face with all the tenacity fingertips can conjure. Once, I felt my weight shifting away from the rock face, as though falling backwards. The point of no return was a matter of inches. Lightning fast, adrenaline kicked in, and I reached for the cliff face, pulling myself flat against it.

I realized this was serious.

I cannot overstate how steep the drop off was behind me. It was a "don't look down" scenario of the highest order. There was a small scaffold far to my right and higher where a Peruvian man was doing restoration work. Upon seeing me, his face revealed his astonishment at the doofus clinging to life. He shouted things to me in Spanish which I assume weren't for a family audience.

Turning back really was not a safer option at that point. I could see the landing area and the backs of some group members.

If I could just get up there.

Finding handholds and footholds wherever I could, I began to climb the 10 or so feet to the landing. "There are no atheists in foxholes" is an expression often used in war. I will admit to having offered my religious loyalty to any god, religion or deity who may have been listening. Living as a Shaman somewhere seemed a fair trade versus becoming goo on the rocks below.

Fortunately, the rock face was more forgiving and less steep. Back pain constant but no longer crippling, I climbed slowly, finally getting to the flat area.

Enormously relieved, I stood up, my volume of sweat far exceeded the temperatures.

The group was standing around with the guide doing a head count, coming up one short. I, from behind him, said, "Right here!" He turned, puzzled and speechless. Watching everyone come through the tunnel, he must have known I hadn't. He shrugged, as though he assumed a miscount.

Our transportation met in a different place after a good walk, 30-40 minutes later. My adrenaline had only recently dropped to somewhat normal levels.

I guess my luck wasn't so bad after all.

One aspect of visiting Machu Picchu that is rarely discussed is how people arrive there. Aguas Caliente is a town serving as the final launching point to the famed ruins. Sitting alongside the swift current of the Urubamba River, Aguas Caliente was very, very small when we were there. With the famed ruins looking down from above, the town had a few restaurants, small inns, stores and the hot springs the town is named for.

People gather there to be taken up to Machu Picchu. There is a climb of over 1,000 feet (305m) between the two. Tourists climb aboard buses to make the short drive to the top. In order to climb such a steep elevation in lumbering buses, switchback roads were built.

If you have not seen them, switchbacks create the definition of a hairpin turn. The road alternates between sharp right and left turns continuously. If the shortest distance between two points is a straight line, switchback roads create the absolute farthest distance between two points.

Big heavy vehicles don't do "mountain steep" very well. Each stretch of road between the turns is a slight gain in elevation—much like Bolivia's "Death Road." The switchbacks leading up to, and down from, Machu Picchu should be much, much wider.

Guardrails? They would be a good idea as well theoretically.

As we drove up, it was obvious there is no vehicle less suited for switchback/hairpin turns than a bus.

To our left, an older couple told us of the elevation sickness they had suffered in Cusco—bad enough they had to be hospitalized for a few days. Machu Picchu sits about 4,000 feet, roughly 1,000m, lower in altitude than Cusco so they expected no further medical issues.

As we made small talk, our bus lurched to a stop. People gasping and screaming snapped me out of the conversation. Every head on the bus turned forward.

Another bus, coming down the mountain, met us literally nose-to-nose after it made a hairpin right turn. Carrying considerable heft, it was remarkable the bus was able to stop and avoid an epically tragic collision. Imagine a hippopotamus charging down a hill and needing to stop instantly.

I was amazed that they had no basic communication system at the top and bottom to avoid these buses having to pass one another. Clearly, it's better for business to move people up and down quickly, but it reeked of greed and poor planning while also being crazy dangerous.

There was a pregnant pause of a couple seconds when both buses slammed on the brakes. Eventually people breathed with a chorus of expressions following. It is interesting hearing common obscenities in foreign accents.

The poor couple to my left may never leave home again.

The "near-death experience" aside, the switchbacks are very unique and a great experience. Imagine the quirky Lombard Street in San Francisco expanded 100 times in size. Add two-way tour bus traffic, and it is suddenly a pay-per-view event.

As our bus careened back-and-forth across the mountain side, I realized our path looked like the little digital dot in the ancient video game Pong.

When we arrived at the top, the perilous ride was quickly forgotten. The long-lost ruins are a patchwork of vibrant green and stone gray. Seeing them was an immediate reset button. We spent two days at the ruins, using the switchback roads four times in total. There were no more "white-knuckle" moments—the first one was plenty.

Machu Picchu is a must see for adventurous travelers. It is one of the world's top tourist destinations—an experience you can only get by seeing it.

As is the road leading to it.

We stood at the top of Huayna Picchu, the famed backdrop to Machu Picchu's ruins.

With an astounding view of a powerfully moving place, we had been atop the summit of the "Young Mountain" for close to an hour. Space at the top is limited and with more people arriving in a steady stream, it was time for us to leave.

My travel compadre Clint suggested we head down. As he walked away to grab his pack, I picked mine up when someone touched my shoulder from behind. I turned to see a panicked, familiar face. A young woman we had met at Machu Picchu the day before said to me urgently "I have to get down to get my medicine *now*. Will you go with me?" Pack in hand already, no questions asked, I answered, "Sure, let's go."

The twenty-something lady held the secret of how desperate the situation was. What medicine? What condition? I knew nothing aside from her asking me to help. She stood about 5'3", similar in size to the Inca who built the "steps" we were about to descend. I stand 6'3" and typically wear a size 14 shoe. Physically, I have more in common with Frankenstein than with the Inca architects. That was a problem.

The Inca were geniuses of construction and very innovative. These ruins were built in an era where construction equipment consisted of "dudes with logs." It was the kind of scenario you encounter when modern-sized people and vehicles use centuries old roads and stairwells. Things just don't fit very well, as we would discover on Bolivia's Death Road days later.

An added factor was that Peru completely lacked the liability concerns that we Americans are swimming in daily. Honestly, it was refreshing. Should people really require signs reminding them that it's dangerous to walk to the edge of the cliff? Or be cautioned that bison are unpredictable wild animals that don't value selfies with humans? Definitely not.

I realized about five steps down that I hadn't alerted Clint to the situation. He was likely turning around at the top wondering where I went. Speaking to guides the day prior, it was noted that there was no search and rescue in that area. If you fell—well that's pretty much it. If you fell and no one noticed, your whereabouts would likely never be known. If I took a bad tumble, Clint would have no idea what happened.

I noticed the steps—where there were actual steps— were very small on the way up. It doesn't matter much when climbing but it does in a rapid descent. Finding a landing spot for a size 14 shoe on a size 7 step was a challenge. Doing it quickly seemed an impossibility. The various agility drills I had done in football or wrestling could have served me well, had they been more recent. There was a lot of "hop and hope" going on.

Fortunately for her, unfortunately for me, she attacked this descent with agility and quickness. She moved like a bullet ricocheting from steps, to boulder, to boulder, to ledge, to boulder and back to steps. Just my luck that I needed to keep pace with a ninja.

The climb to the top took somewhere between an hour and a half to two hours, with no impetus to hurry. The race track she had me on would *at least* cut that time in half going down.

Adrenaline is powerful. There are countless tales of adrenalized humans doing things thought to be impossible. As I jumped about trying to keep up, I was aware of feeling both invincible and completely aware of the danger. The absolute best-case scenario if I were to get hurt, was a sprained ankle. This was crazy dangerous for both of us, particularly for the Bigfoot lumbering downhill.

There were steel cables to use as handrails in a couple of places and were badly needed in those spots. Most of the time there was nothing to hold onto. The rock face of the mountain was on my left to use if needed, but it offered little to grab ahold of.

On two occasions the steps were so steep and small that I felt my weight shift further forward than I could control and things got real scary. Luck and arms waving wildly got me through it. My heart was pounding.

Another time, when the descent involved rocks and boulders in lieu of steps, I needed to half step/half leap down onto a boulder. Momentum would have made stopping on it unrealistic and it was really too small to stand on. That forced me to immediately take a small leap down to another landing spot to gather my wits. A lot could have gone wrong there.

Complicating this further was the flow of people going up. It's hard to hurry down this terrain, while not going over the edge, if you are there all alone. Doing so, while in two-way foot traffic was another thing altogether. That often meant having to move to the right and lose the rock face as an ally. Some stretches were perilous, others not so bad.

Five days earlier, I was lying on the airport terminal floor with bad back spasms and now, here I was, imitating a mountain goat. The lady I was "helping" looked back on occasion to check my progress. I did not maintain her pace, falling farther behind but not losing sight of her for long stretches.

I eventually got to the bottom huffing and puffing like a congested race horse. She was drinking something and a pill bottle was in the hand of the guy she was with. She walked toward me and said, "Thanks so much. It was helpful knowing you were there." She gave me the cordial "half hug" customary for people you know but don't actually *know*. Gasping for air, I responded, "No Prah, (heh, heh, heh) blem glad, (heh, heh, heh) to (heh, heh) help," five words that seemed like five paragraphs.

He nodded toward me, and they walked off. I didn't see them again.

I am sure I was quite a sight.

This was July, winter in Peru. It was in the low 50s F (11 C). The altitude alone made hustling a chore. All I wanted to do was simply stop. Just sit down and be done. A sweaty mess despite cool temps, I sat on a boulder, while my heart pounded, and relived the events of the past 30-45 minutes. A couple of protein bars and a water bottle later, I thought of the marathons I had run. *n-o-t-h-i-n-g* sounds better to a marathon runner during a race than just sitting down.

This felt better than that.

Not because of exhaustion—marathons are physically tougher. Mentally though, this was quite a ride. I sat there for a long stint watching people from all over the world pass by. The variety of languages spoken reminded me how international the visitors to Machu Picchu are.

Clint and I were among the first group up Huayna Picchu that morning. Arriving at the top, we were there with six other people. Two young guys from Queensland, Australia, celebrated by waving a flag above the mystical ruins of the Inca. There was a couple from Namibia and two Germans as well.

Lost in thought, I was snapped out of it by Clint's familiar voice, saying, "There you are!" I stood up, smiled and shook my head saying, "You have no idea . . ."

If I were to visit Machu Picchu again, there is no doubt I would hike the Inca Trail. When we arrived to the ruins our first day, there were people just arriving via the hike. I spoke to a few of them and could see how deeply moved they were by the experience.

We all stared at the ruins in amazement, like a high school freshman views the homecoming queen.

I had seen the ruins in pictures only and arrived not a bit disappointed.

Seeing pictures of anything before seeing it in person, dilutes the experience a tiny bit. I suppose it would be better if you only *heard* a fabulous place described.

Imagine the first person to see Lake Louise near Banff in Canada. It's stunning to see in person even after looking at a dozen pictures of it. To have stumbled upon it—the first to ever see it—would be beyond description.

It was obvious that those who had hiked the Inca Trail were getting a larger pay off. Perhaps it was the anticipation, or the effort involved in getting there.

Camping among the majestic Andes would be a memorable experience as a stand-alone trip. Arriving at Machu Picchu afterward could only be amazing. There are different lengths of hikes available. Half a week through two weeks can be easily found with experienced guides.

Sherpas, among the most admirable, hard-working people on the planet, do all the dirty work. I'm not sure I could allow a Sherpa to carry my bags for me.

Don't misunderstand, I am happy for them to earn a substantial amount of money.

I would feel guilty subjugating another person to carry something that I can carry far more easily myself.

Even when I had searing back pain on the trip to Peru, I carried my bags. Very rarely does an airport shuttle driver lift my bag for me. If so, he got to my bag quicker than I could.

I am 6'3" and 200 pounds. This is not big by American football standards, yet I tower over the majority of men in developing countries. If the word Sherpa was used as a measurement tool, like feet or meters, I would stand about 1 1/4 Sherpas tall and I'd weigh in at about 1 1/2 Sherpas.

I have run a dozen marathons with years of wrestling experience and played football through college. I've dead lifted, bench pressed and power cleaned. Why should I, in good conscience, hand my bag to someone the size of a jockey? I don't put that stance onto others, it is just how I am wired.

That may just be a view particular to me. As I watch other people allowing employees to carry their bags, it looks completely normal. By the final day of the Inca Trail hike, I am sure there are many who are thrilled that the Sherpas are doing a lot of the work.

Over a decade has passed since my visit to Machu Picchu. That time has not dulled the allure of hiking the Inca Trail to the ruins at all.

To the contrary, the desire may have grown.

Cusco, sometimes spelled Cuzco, is one of my favorite places. When raving about one place, compared to another, it's important to remember it is an issue of personal preference.

Some people love a modern metropolis, others a small village somewhat behind the times. Certainly everyone wouldn't love Cusco as much as I did.

Sitting at 11,000ft (3,300m) above sea level, it is much higher than the elevation boundary of 8,000ft (2400m) where altitude sickness can be a factor. We were fortunate to have no problems.

Cusco was originally built by the Inca tribe and served as the capital of their empire. When the gold-seeking Spaniards arrived, they left their mark on Cusco. It looks very European. Quaint, narrow streets spill into the town square called the Plaza de Armas.

Cathedrals in that area are as common as drug stores in the U.S.

The legal drug stores, to be clear.

We stayed in a small hotel right on the plaza. The rooms were nothing special, but the location was hard to beat.

Visiting in July, the South American winter, it was coat weather for sure but fairly pleasant. Temperatures ranged from the 30s to 50s F (0-12 C).

After dark, Cusco, particularly the Plaza de Armas, takes on a real vibrancy. It is not a big place, but the lights of the city dominate the darkness that surrounds it.

We had dinner one night on the second-floor balcony of a café that overlooked the Plaza. As the sunlight disappeared behind the gigantic mountains surrounding Cusco, we noticed small lights here and there speckled throughout total darkness on the mountains.

A waiter explained that those were fires used as light and heat sources by some of the Peruvian people living nearby.

Many of the restaurants and cafés had live music but not the type of the modern music festival. The musicians we heard were playing a very local type of music passed down by the indigenous tribes.

One night after dinner, a three-man group began playing. The music was traditional Peruvian, and it definitely lent a mystique to an impressive place.

As they played, we enjoyed a few drinks and struck up a conversation with two Swedish women sitting next to us.

They were very attractive and had just come from a stint in the Galapagos islands. These ladies were totally into the guys performing. The allure of a vocalist and guitarist is apparently global.

We took some guided tours of the surrounding Sacred Valley which was phenomenal to take in. The Andes mountains, like the Rockies, can amaze you. Closer in, around Cusco, you would see big letters here and there facing outward on many mountainsides like the "Hollywood" sign. Typically, these were just two letters, and usually white.

I asked a guide what those letters were for. He said those were the initials of the high school in that given area. The roads being so windy, and GPS so primitive then, those letters were actually used as a way for people to find the school. Coming from a country where every kid seems to get picked up by a school bus, it reminded me how different people live from place to place.

And how generally spoiled people are in the U.S.

One day we walked around the area and found a school just a block or two from the plaza. Clint and I being teachers, we were genuinely intrigued.

As you would expect, in an area where some people still use fire for light and heat, the school was horribly equipped by the standards of the developed world. The marching band's 15 or so members practiced nearby doing the best they could with what they had.

I felt bad for those kids having so little.

The only negative of our days in Cusco was the number of children begging for handouts, particularly money.

I wish they didn't have to, and understand their plight. This appeared to be an orchestrated maneuver by local adults. Sending children into the fray will certainly yield a bigger return. If a tourist gave anything to a child, they were swarmed by others.

It is easy to feel guilty as an American traveling around the world. Though America has plenty of poverty, it showcases obscene wealth—not always in good ways. Around the year 2000, I saw a statistic that showed the average American household making $60,000 a year or more was one of the 5% wealthiest in the world.

That says a lot more about the poverty outside the U.S. than it does about the value of $60,000.

On our last day in Peru I went to a street vendor to buy a bottle of water. It is wise to check the cap and see that it has not been opened previously. I have not encountered that problem, but it's not unheard of for a bottle to be refilled and resold in poor countries.

The man was asking me for one Peruvian peso in exchange for the water. I had already exchanged my Peruvian money and only had U.S. dollars. The exchange rate was eight Peruvian pesos for one U.S. dollar.

I handed one dollar to the man, then gestured with one hand for him to keep the change. The gratitude he showed for me giving him an 88 cent bonus stuck with me. It was such a small amount of money, yet it was an unexpected bonus for him; and he was extraordinarily thankful.

As we prepared to leave Peru and enter Bolivia, we had one last thing to accomplish.

We had made arrangements to take a boat out into Lake Titicaca. The target was a group of inhabited islands in the lake that are made of reeds.

The plans got messy, but we worked it out and got on the boat early in the morning. On this boat, I was reminded it was winter in the southern hemisphere.

Temperatures in the 30s felt far colder due to the winds on the lake. The boat's impressive speed made it all the worse. This was not the type of boat that had a cabin below deck. No sir. This was a "sit and deal with it" situation.

A decade later, I am extraordinarily glad we did it. That day, after about 30 minutes of cold wind it seemed like the worst idea ever.

Though I hate cold, clearly many love it, otherwise animals would be the lone inhabitants of Canada. Each time I complain about cold experiences, I realize how wimpy modern society is, particularly in the developed world.

The soldiers on both sides of the Battle of the Bulge in World War II, at the peak of one of the coldest winters on record, were out in the elements day and night for six straight weeks.

In World War I, German troops came across a Russian camp where thousands of soldiers died during the winter night from exposure. The horridly cold boat ride on Lake Titicaca would likely have felt like a resort to those poor soldiers.

When I was really young, a big storm hit St. Louis and our elementary school had a "snow day." *Nothing* is better to a kid than a snow day. It was single-digits cold and windy and we had gotten over 10 inches of snow. From the front of our house, I could see a good portion of the street.

No one was outside.

Cabin fever set in quickly and I asked my mom if I could explore outside. Her answer of, "No, it's too cold" created a series of protests. Being peppered with complaints and whining was like being pecked to death by a duck. No single comment was painful, but they came in an overwhelming barrage.

She caved and bundled me up to the extreme. I had a coat with a hood that would zip up past my top lip. The faux fur-trimmed hood, when tied shut, created a portal. Looking at me, all one could see was two blue eyes and a nose.

I waddled outside, feeling braver than most. Soon my nose began to run. If dealing with cold isn't bad enough, that side effect is particularly annoying. As a boy, it may be charming. As an adult, it's just gross.

I snorted that back up into my nose over and over. Wearing mittens the size of catchers' mitts made dealing with it a challenge. Continuously, it would run down toward my lip and I would retrieve it like a yo-yo. After having been outside long enough to **feel** the cold, I again sniffed the escaping goo up to where it belonged. This time, my nostrils stayed shut. Frozen there. There was no release, no re-opening. My mom was right—it was too cold.

Breathing from my mouth was not easy since it was zipped up inside the coat. I panicked! Waddling around looking through my portal, I knew I was going to die right there. I'd be found frozen on the driveway like a blue-eyed hockey puck. Bravery be damned, I hurried to the door and banged on it. My mom, being the best, was watching me through the window. She opened the door and helped me unzip and untie the hood. Mouth free and clear, breathing came easy.

Within seconds, my nostrils popped open and life was great again. Staying inside was noooooo issue the rest of the day. Me and cold still don't get along.

The ride on Lake Titicaca reminded me of that. Eventually we got to the islands. The frigid ride was worth the experience. Land made of reeds cannot be solid. Imagine living on land so soft each step felt like walking on a water bed.

Part of these people's daily lives was adding reeds to the top of the island. As those on the bottom deteriorated into nothing, the top of the island became the bottom in time.

From any of these islands you could easily see eight to ten neighboring islands, constructed the same way. Atop these islands were huts the people lived in.

One island had a larger structure on it. The guide told us it was the school the children attended. Unlike children walking, busing or driving to school, these kids rowed canoes to school and back every day.

The islands were a unique experience. Far-fetched enough to sound like a drunken dream and well worth the time, money and potential frostbite. They were the kind of thing one can only experience by traveling to faraway places.

As nutty as people living on islands made of reeds may sound, the most far-fetched experience of my life awaited me in Bolivia. A drive of several hours through the Andes Mountains on a highway known around the world as The Death Road awaited. We just had to check it out.

CHAPTER 3 - BOLIVIA

Clint and I arrived in Bolivia via the charming town of Copacabana, perched on the edge of Lake Titicaca. The gorgeous blue hues of the lake, whose name made me giggle in middle school, triggered memories of our visit to the reed islands earlier in the trip. When one's body temperature drops below that of a corpse, it's kind of hard to forget.

Fighting off the corresponding urge to buy blankets, we walked through the small town of several thousand people. Street markets sold nearly everything in bright, vivid colors. We visited a cathedral older than the U.S. It was seemingly the 4,000[th] cathedral we had seen on the trip.

This was my first glimpse of a church service in a foreign country. Mass had already started, yet things were very different than I expected.

My earliest experiences during childhood are where "normal" was established in my head. My incredible parents are both Christian but of differing denominations. My mom is Catholic, my dad Baptist. Early on as kids, we spent time going to both churches each Sunday. We were taught to be quiet, with no monkeybusiness in church and we tried to comply. We dressed well and sat respectfully quiet throughout Mass.

For a fidgety kid, Catholicism was incredible. Shifting from sitting to kneeling to standing throughout the Mass broke up the monotony. The priest often talked about the St. Louis Cardinals football team during Mass which, of course, impressed me. The Baptist service didn't have the built-in noise and movement the Catholic Mass provided. People scattered around the church bellowed out "*Amen*" again and again. *This was a thing*, yet somehow, I knew it wouldn't go over well if I tried it. The pastor at the Baptist church was a friendly, charismatic friend of the family that I looked up to.

To a kid just old enough to start attending school, I noticed differences between the two denominations. Each was different to me based on my experience, but normal in its own context.

Twenty years later, a high school athlete I coached was tragically killed in a drive by shooting. A group of students and coaches attended the funeral at a Pentecostal church in the inner city.

I knew a couple of things may happen in the service that I had not seen in person. Church members "speaking in tongues" and people occasionally falling to the floor, feeling the power of God in them, are routine within Pentecostal walls. I forgot to prep the athletes about what they may likely be seeing for the first time.

A lady sitting near our group had a religious experience. Standing up, arms raised above her head, eyes shut, she shimmied from head to toe, speaking in tongues. Several of our young men sitting in front of us rubber-necked toward me, heads seemingly spinning 180 degrees in astonishment, "wide-eyed" in an environment they had never before experienced. She collapsed to the floor, and congregation members tended to her. Fifteen minutes later, the lady was fine, as though nothing had happened.

The students were full of questions on the drive home. They had been introduced to a religion different from theirs, an example of how life experiences are crucial to shaping well-rounded people.

Those religions have significantly different customs in some ways. Yet, they are merely different doorways found in the house of Christianity. Sister religions, but different. Many churches in the U.S. have now modernized" and offer an almost concert-like experience. The services carry a message while also being entertaining along the way. These changes are parallel to the societal shift toward shorter attention spans— keeping pace with shifts that video rental and record stores wish they could have.

Knowing that, I shouldn't have been surprised by the casualness of the Mass in Copacabana.

The only ambient noise congregations from my childhood dealt with was the wailing of babies. It was tolerated until the embarrassed parent could hustle the unhappy minion to another room. Many churches created separate rooms for parents with young babies, where they could see and hear the proceedings, without the shrieking disrupting the atmosphere of respect. It was clear that the church wanted silence.

Many of the Bolivians in attendance were dressed well—normal from my experiences. Others were very casual. A man in workout clothes sat on his bike near a sidewall of the cathedral. A line of tourists filed around the perimeter of the church during Mass, reading plaques and admiring sculptures. The congregation was largely quiet, tolerating a murmur of noise from those sightseeing.

Though I thought they could easily close the cathedral to sightseeing during masses, they chose not to. The priest carried on through the Mass despite the lack of attention and quiet from some. This was normal to him. On my first international trip, I was barraged with "different being normal." An oxymoron, yet true at the same time.

A driver picked us up to drive to La Paz, Bolivia's capitol. The ride lasted a little longer than three hours. There wasn't much conversation as we digested the incredible Bolivian countryside.

The church atmosphere had surprised me, but a bigger shock to my "normalcy" awaited. As we arrived in La Paz, the city looked very familiar, and amazingly chaotic, all at once. The roads had lane lines painted and modern stoplights. Street signs looked familiar, aside from the Spanish words on them. The government had invested in a first-world traffic infrastructure, yet all of those elements were wildly ignored.

Sitting at a huge intersection "regulated" by stop lights, the drivers treated the signs and lights as polite suggestions they could ignore. Lane lines? No one paid attention to them either. It was a massive vehicular mosh pit.

Folks in cars and trucks separated by the thinnest of margins could have "high-fived" the people beside them. Had Godzilla shown up, it would have been the most orderly disaster movie ever. No one could open their doors enough to get out and run, nor could they speed off.

Cars from all directions crept forward. Progress was slower than mine in algebra class. The car would move approximately "two Sherpas" forward every five minutes. The utter insanity was complicated by cars in the left lane trying to turn right and things of that ilk.

The police sat by calmly.

If a community ever wanted to prank their police, this was a beautiful plan. Overwhelm them with people committing as many traffic violations as possible, all in one intersection. Even if they chose to try and restore order, their vehicles would be absolutely glued in place by the ones around them.

The uptight U.S. citizen part of me wanted to climb on the hood of the car and yell, *"Alright! Everybody listen up!"* and then start directing traffic in an orderly fashion, taking turns as we learned in second grade. In La Paz, there were very few horns or signs of discontent. This was their normal.

Road rage is common in the U.S., yet, in a country with good roads and relative total conformity to road laws, what is there to "rage" about? Judges in the United

States should sentence those guilty of road rage to drive endlessly through La Paz for 48 hours.

I would love to sit about 10 floors above that fray and watch the angry American completely implode—going berserk on unsuspecting Bolivian drivers, his face as red as a baboon's backside, spitting while he screams at everyone around him.

Gesturing wildly, he would be throwing his hands in the air while cussing out everyone in sight. The calm Bolivians would look at him completely baffled. He would honk and make a fool of himself acting like everyone else was the problem until possibly passing out from screaming too much.

That thought made me chuckle as I watched the proceedings around me. If organized mayhem is possible, this was it. We eventually reached our hotel after traveling through La Paz at a slothian pace.

We entered Bolivia with no concrete plans but wanted to end this trip in style. Clint walked into the hotel room and asked, "What do you think about this?" He had a brochure in his hand titled *"The Worlds' Most Dangerous Highway."*

That easily our plans were made.

Why was this appealing? I suppose I was a little skeptical that it was really *that* dangerous. Coming from the U.S. where liability concerns are supersized, I assumed this couldn't be what the brochure claimed.

And I love scary things.

Most of them.

If we were tramping about India, you'd never hear me say "Hey is that a cobra? Let's go see! In Florida, people routinely paddleboard on lakes full of gators. I'll pass. We all have our "things." I leapt at the chance to scuba dive in Hawaii and loved every bit of a skydive in New Zealand. Plenty of people thought I was daft for both.

I am entertained by the fact people love scary things. A creepy book or movie around Halloween just feels right to that crowd.

As a kid, I read Dracula, and The Amityville Horror in succession. Both were page turners. I would go outside to play but be drawn back to those books quickly. It was a burrito of fascination and terror. Around the same time, I watched Hitchcock's *Psycho*. No elementary-aged twerp should do any of those things.

At night, I would lie awake in bed, eyes bugging wide thinking about all of the awful things that could happen. The closet was a menace, and lord knew what was under the bed. Was Jody, the red-eyed, imaginary pig from Amityville_peering in my window?

As a kid, I loved having the attic fan pull a breeze over me, so I positioned my bed directly under that window. If Jodi was looking in, I wouldn't notice. Kid logic, right?

Until I saw the movie, *Salem's Lot*.

A scene showed a young vampire scratching on the bedroom window of a friend. I changed the layout of my room immediately. Had I owned the house, I would have boarded up my window and planted garlic right below it. The bed was permanently moved.

I would read, get scared, lie awake scared, then eagerly read more until the books were done. It was a strange desire to further one's own misery, much like travelers who journey down "The World's Most Dangerous Highway."

The Bolivians call it "El Camino de la Muerte" which charmingly translates to "The Death Road." As the world heard of it, travelers came from all over. It is Bolivia's most famous attraction. For over two decades there have been companies leading bicycle and car tours of The Death Road. Mountain bikers, a fearless breed, see biking The Death Road as a "must."

Naturally, a footrace has been created with runners racing up 28 lung-popping kilometers, then cycling down afterwards.

Like the eight-year-old who pulls a blanket over his head when he hears something at night, I am certain many of those cycling The Death Road have the adrenaline of fear pumping through them. They knew they would be scared, or worse, yet they came.

The Death Road will never attract the casual traveler. It cannot be photographed from a distance like the Eiffel Tower and other monuments.

To see The Death Road, you must travel it.

Soon after Clint made the arrangements, we met the driver and guide. The trip would take us down the road, to a hacienda for an overnight stay, then return the next day. The driver was experienced on this road but spoke little English. The friendly guide spoke when necessary, but luckily not as though he was paid by the word.

La Paz is over 8,000ft (2400m) *higher* than Denver. Elevations like that of La Paz are incredibly serene settings. Living at over 13,000ft (4,000m) above sea level places you in a nest among massive mountains, with snow and rain ensuring that plant life is vibrant.

Even while on the Death Road, the valley below is incredibly lush, though jumbled heaps of trucks, cars and buses make it more macabre than scenic.

Just before entering The Death Road, we saw several cycling outfitters getting the next legion of daredevils geared up. Within minutes, several things were immediately clear. The surface was pockmarked with gravel, dirt and potholes. It wasn't a bumpy ride throughout, but we spent plenty of time as bobble heads.

The road certainly felt like a vehicular version of walking a tight rope. Steep cliff walls to one side, and an equally steep drop off on the other, framed the ride.

The North Yungas Highway is the official name, Yungas being a region in Northern Bolivia.

Let's define what a "highway" is. My definition includes 70 mph speed limits, and a minimum of two lanes in each direction, with those lanes preferably divided.

I have been annoyed on road trips in the U.S. when a scenic "highway" turns out to be a country road. Some of them are enjoyable jaunts through farmland, though, invariably, fate puts me behind a tractor with a top speed of a souped-up tricycle.

America's skinniest farm road is a wonderland of space compared to Bolivia's Death Road. Before being "built out" into a highway, The Death Road was originally a mule path.

Yes, a mule path.

While never a full two-lane width anywhere along the route, the Death Road is *only a single lane width* in places. Yet, it has traffic in two directions.

Complicating things is the constantly winding path the road takes. From a "bird's-eye" view the highway would look like a massive brown snake, twisting and curling to the whim of the Andes range. Rare is a stretch of the road that is truly straight for the length of a futbol field. The number of blind turns outpaced my ability to count, which, admittedly, is a weakness.

The road begins in the neighborhood of 15,000ft (4500m) above sea level, near La Paz. The North Yungas Highway descends down to the Amazon River basin over its 30 mile plus length. It had been, until 2006, the only source of supplies for towns sitting alongside it.

The Death Road is skinny, with two-way traffic and blind turns. One can see how it got its reputation, right?

We haven't gotten to the good stuff yet.

In the rainy season, there is thick, soupy fog, making *every* turn, a blind one. Adding to the fun, are scattered waterfalls splashing down *on* the road.

In fairness, we are talking a trickle of water compared to Niagara Falls. You drive over most of the water; an occasional splatter may hit the top of the car. The waterfalls, powered by snow melt and rain, turn the dirt surface into mud and this hinders traction.

How important can traction possibly be when going the speed of your great-grandfather's scooter? Ubiquitous in the developed world, you definitely notice the *lack* of guardrails when skirting the very edge of the road. Traction is vital.

On a two-way road, with all of those challenges, the Bolivian people developed ways of minimizing risk. One adaptation was driving on the left. That puts the driver going downhill, away from La Paz, on the outer edge of the road.

The *very outer edge.*

In one instance where another vehicle and ours passed in opposite directions, I was seated behind the driver and raised up and tried to peer down at the roads edge. The edge *was directly under the tires.*

Another strategy deals with "right-of-way." If the road is too narrow for vehicles to pass aside each other, the downhill driver has to *back up* on this road until finding a spot wide enough for the other car to pass. Backing up around blind turns, then snuggling up to the very outer edge is a *real thing* on this road. We stopped several times and walked to the edge. It was literally a straight drop down in places

In spots, where you could see a sharp turn coming up, a local man, rewarded by tips, would stand on the outer edge holding up a long pole with a red or green circle on the end. If he showed you the red side, there was a car coming on the other side of the blind turn. He wasn't an employee—just a local solving a problem.

Almost immediately upon entering the Death Road, there was a large roadside memorial. It was paid for by the country of Israel in honor of Israelis who died when a tour bus went over the edge in the 1990s. I could not imagine a tour bus on this road.

Roadside memorials are common in most countries. Small and heartfelt, they always remind me how quickly things can go tragically awry. Along the Death Road small memorials were everywhere. At each one, our driver would cross himself out of respect.

There were several locations where the guide would tell stories of accidents with large death tolls. He did so appropriately, respectful of the sad overtone. The driver subtly made the sign of the cross probably 40 or 50 times on our nearly three-hour drive.

Bolivia, in 2004, didn't have tractor trailer semi-trucks like we see in the U.S. They used big Volvo trucks to move freight. We came nose-to-nose with one of those around a blind turn.

Our small SUV being the downhill vehicle, we had to back up to a spot where the truck could pass. I am sure having passengers in the backseat didn't help the driver navigate the winding edge. He used the driver's mirror.

From behind him, my angle was admittedly different. Seeing a strip of road skinnier than a guinea pig between the tires and certain death, he slowly backed up maybe 200 meters, equal to half a lap on a high school track.

The "wide spot" where he stopped didn't seem *nearly* wide enough. Placed on the very edge of the road, on the left, we watched as the hulking truck tried to pass by on our right. If I had opened my door, I would have been looking straight down the cliff. Had the Volvo truck bumped us slightly, our left wheels may have been pushed off the road.

The truck shimmied by with its side mirror not being beside ours, but above it. *Inches* separated the two vehicles. I really wasn't that worried, figuring these drivers do this daily. Our driver was less confident, again doing the sign of the cross. The truck passed, *incredibly slowly*, and we continued along.

A few miles later, our guide pointed to a spot in the road, well ahead of us. This part of the road was particularly crooked. The specific place he pointed out was like an elbow in the road before it made a sharp right turn. This spot was in the sun, while most surrounding it was shaded. The guide told us that a Bolivian dictator had once used that spot as a place to execute prisoners. They would be blindfolded, then pushed off.

We encountered a few more vehicles and had to back up again. These encounters weren't as harrowing but still made you realize the difficulties of daily life in this area.

Let's recap, the North Yungas Highway is skinny, with two-way traffic, blind turns, fog, waterfalls, mud and a scarcity of guardrails.

Oh, and there are rock slides.

Sometimes a solo boulder tumbles down, sometimes groups of them. That's a nice touch. Drive slowly and carefully, honoring the rules of the road, cautiously looking down at the road's edge, only to be fly-swatted by falling boulders.

There is really only one horrible element missing.

Of course—Nazi's.

In need of assistance on the North Yungas Highway, what a comfort it must have been to spot a house, the only one for miles. You knock on the door and Klaus Barbie, a man the French called the "Butcher of Lyon," opens the door. Fitting that such a man had an address on The Death Road.

Barbie was a fugitive WWII criminal guilty of torturing and murdering people from his base of operation in Lyon, France. We were told that Barbie would occasionally go to clubs in La Paz wearing his Nazi dress uniform, very proud of that status. He lived there under the protection of a Bolivian dictator, likely assisting the government in interrogation and torture. After that dictator was deposed, Barbie was turned over to the French by the new, more liberal government in the 1980's and died in prison several years later.

So yes, for a time, The Death Road also had a Nazi.

Before long we came to that house—the lone one we had seen thus far. It was perched on the right in total isolation, exactly what a fugitive Nazi would have needed. Seeing that house was interesting—kind of like looking at a house where a murder had been committed.

The Amityville house, made famous during my childhood, had a unique look. The window design and house shape stood out. People of my generation would likely recognize it immediately. The Nazi house on The Death Road looked very homogenous, a typical one-story ranch design. Recently, I stumbled upon a picture of that house, with no caption identifying it. I recognized it immediately.

The drive back the next day felt "brand new". Driving uphill, we hugged the cliff face and had no "white knuckle" moments. I did notice many interesting facial expressions in passing cars flirting with the edge. People with mouths agape, likely selling *their* loyalty to any religious deity offering safe passage. The North Yungas Highway is unlike any road I had ever seen. An experience to be sure.

We returned from The Death Road feeling victorious but not unscathed. The previous day, after arriving at the hacienda, both of us started to feel sick. Then it got worse.

We all feel awful at times, and know it will pass. I am not sure how universal my thoughts are when I am sick, but there are times I want the entire roof to collapse, just to end the misery. Being sick in a developing country is even worse. Potentially inaccurate, your mind still leaps to hospitals with a single light bulb swinging back and forth over the operating table.

The surgical team chuckles in a foreign language as they prep you for surgery. You see instruments that appear to be from the era of the U.S. Civil War and a bottle of whiskey is the anesthesia.

Fortunately, by the next day, we felt fine.

As travel guides always suggest, we had avoided drinking from glasses, using ice, or eating fruits and vegetables that may have been washed in the water. Comparing meals that day, we realized there was only one thing we both had consumed. After surviving all of the quirks and pitfalls of The Death Road, we were both done in by yogurt.

We were flying back to the U.S. the next day. I needed to hatch a plan to deal with the long day of travel. The book I brought with me was finished. I had taken more pictures on the trip than the Hubble Space Telescope. With all of that film to lug, I figured getting it devel-

PEANUT BUTTER AND PASSPORTS

oped made sense. I could sort photos, and make notes, on the flight home.

Clint warned me against it—noting that the developing world, ironically, can struggle at developing. Dreading boredom, I could either take the chance or hope the Bolivian airport sold books in English.

We found a Fuji film store.

The next ten minutes were comedy gold. The smiling young lady trying to help me, spoke nothing but Spanish, whereas, I speak Spanish as deftly as a raccoon. I think we both enjoyed the continually failing combo of speaking and charades. Each time either of us spoke, it was with a laugh.

Not surprisingly, Fuji anticipated people like me traveling to Spanish-speaking countries with a Mexican restaurant vocabulary. The countertop was full of menus, pictures and prices. The employee pointed to them and our entertaining attempts to communicate were resolved. The photos turned out just fine.

We arrived at the airport the next day. Feeling smart, I found a bookstore to confirm my belief that all of the books would be in Spanish. Surrounding me were dozens of options printed in English. Realizing people had actually traveled internationally before I did and

88

figured all of this out, I felt stupid for having such a narrow view of the world. Another lesson learned about traveling worldwide—any issue or problem has been dealt with countless times before.

I have encountered some strange circumstances on airplanes, and in airports. My next trip to Cuba involved many of them. Not a flight delay or a fugitive Nazi, but a very unusual "hostage" situation that made at least one member of the Miami police department laugh.

CHAPTER 4 - CUBA

After returning from the trip to South America, I didn't leave the U.S. again for 11 years. Most of that time was a career focus. The teaching and coaching career was at its apex in the decade after leaving the U.S. for the first time.

There were a lot of domestic trips in that stint. I was awestruck at the grandeur witnessed during my first visits to Colorado, California and all through the Rocky Mountains. Jaunts to Chicago, Providence, Las Vegas and assorted other great destinations kept me on the go.

I got married at age 40 and divorced six years later. I learned a lot about myself, my shortcomings and what I needed to work on as a person. I totally respect my ex-wife and will always wish her the very best. She deserves a great life.

Less than a year after my divorce in October, 2015 my friend Mark texted me. the question. "Do you want to go to Cuba in January, for free?"—a question that required no deliberation. The following January, a long holiday weekend in the U.S., we would journey to Havana for three days.

Or so we thought.

Half of the approximately 80 travelers in our group were teachers that take student groups on international trips organized by a tour company named ACIS. This trip to Cuba was a "thank you" to the teachers from the company. The other half of our group were categorized as "plus 1s," or lucky blokes that had friends or spouses who had done the hard work so we could tag along.

I was a bloke.

At orientation in Miami on Friday morning, we were told to "roll with the punches" regarding times and itineraries. Much of it was beyond our control from that point forward.

It was a prescient warning. Our flight was scheduled to leave at 1pm. It was nearly departure time, and we hadn't boarded yet. The ACIS staff, all friendly, poised and highly professional, spread the word that the pilot was sick. Our flight was delayed while another pilot was located.

The large group was very excited about visiting Cuba. It felt like we had permission to visit a forbidden place. Due to the trip being a cultural exchange, we were getting into Cuba ahead of many of the famous names in the travel industry. I heard no grousing. We patiently mingled and got to know one another.

A couple of hours later, we were called to board. About 20 people boarded, then immediately came right back off. The airplane had been hit by lightning en route to Miami and needed repairs. We had a pilot, now we needed a plane. The ACIS staff delivered the bad news, adding that "this would be a while." The trip being just three days long, delays dissolved a significant chunk of the time spent on the mysterious Island. The group remained upbeat.

It was the best delay ever.

I said to a group near us "Who wants to find a restaurant?" With that, a smattering of total strangers headed off and made the best of it for hours. It was incredible getting to know one another. The size of the gathering ranged from seven to double that, as people came and went. Mark and I emceed a travel-related roundtable that passed the time quickly. Food and drinks made grumpiness completely vanish.

Sometime around the confluence of evening and night, the group received an update. We had a pilot and a plane however; the airport was now closed due to a storm. This was a *major* hit to our compact trip. I was pleasantly surprised that there was no overt complaining. Hotel beds sounded good to a lot of people— particularly those sleeping in terminals with their mouths wide open.

The flight was at 7am the next morning and called for a 5am departure from the hotel. A voice from the back of the pack asked a great question, "What about our bags?" The ACIS crew told the group to head back to the hotel we stayed at the previous night. Shuttles were waiting, and our suitcases would be in the hotel lobby when we awoke.

The Great Cuban Suitcase Caper started after 10pm. With a storm raging wildly enough to close an airport, it seemed logical that the airport crew may need to wait until *after* the storm to off-load the luggage from the plane.

There is always someone who disagrees.

Suddenly there were police talking to our tour leaders. A person in the group thought their suitcase was being "held hostage" and alerted the authorities. Apparently, the police were able to assure the person there was no sinister luggage conspiracy.

People-watching is a favorite pastime of mine. I have long wished I could look at people and a "thought bubble" would rise above their head to reveal their details. If so, I could look at a balding guy with disheveled hair, a baggy suit, white gym socks with dress shoes and see his summary. "Accountant, scrabble-lover, two cats, loves opera. Married to Wilma, a seamstress, who records, and binge-watches Jeopardy"

I work out at a gym daily, and there is no more fertile place for people watching. I used to see a guy who would alternate doing a set of weight training with reading a book. Eight reps of an exercise, then read a page. Or half a chapter. He got a lot more reading done than lifting.

I have also seen men wearing sleeveless shirts or tank tops at the gym, exposing a gorilla pelt of sweaty back and shoulder hair. Think Chewbacca with a Celtics jersey. Though there is some dignity to loving the body you have, there is far more dignity to wearing sleeves if you shed.

There was a lady that clearly made up her training regimen. I know weight training in depth—this wasn't it. It looked more like a mating dance on Animal Planet, involving dumbbells and pulleys. I thought a hidden camera show was trying to catch my reaction.

Extreme grunters, weight-slamming meatheads and men wearing skin-tight shirts that shouldn't, are sprinkled throughout. I have seen people on stationary bikes flapping their arms like wings. There are people on stair climbers who bob left and right so much I almost get motion sickness watching them.

It would have been fascinating to know those people's details, just to match up my guess with the real truth. Watching people deal with difficult travel circumstances adds a layer of interest. Luggage being "held hostage" is people-watching gold.

If a trip has to be disrupted by bad luck, it is good to have ACIS in charge of the details. I asked one of their tour leaders how they planned to get all of the luggage back to three different hotels? She replied, "We will take care of it."

"We" consisted of four highly competent ladies. With 80 travelers, a conservative guess tallied 120 suitcases to wrangle from carousels. And that was the easy part. The luggage then had to be cross-checked off rosters, sorted by hotel and then loaded and delivered to three locations. It was a complete "no-brainer" for Mark and I to stay and help. It was decided without it being discussed. Two other men, liaisons with the Cuban end of the trip, pitched in too.

As the group disappeared to the waiting shuttles, the eight of us stayed to deliver the hostages, sorry . . . the luggage . . . back to the hotels. I finally got to bed a little after 3am. After less than two hours of sleep, we headed back to resume our journey. I am not a night owl. At all. I wondered if this long slog of a day would haunt me later in the trip

Excited to *finally* leave Miami, the group arrived at the airport. Three days in Cuba would now be two, and we arrived at the gate to more bad news.

The airport was closed due to fog.

Mark is a really funny, great guy who has traveled all over and when he gets bored things happen. He decided to start a betting pool. For a $5 ante, whoever guessed closest to the "wheels up" time won the pot. Word got around and people got involved from all over the terminal. Two new friends, teachers from Iowa, held the loot and distributed it. These ladies were a lot of fun and were behind considerable shenanigans. The winner pocketed several hundred dollars. We left the U.S. around 1 pm.

Arriving in a communist country, one would expect some differences. There was certainly never anything

menacing. The airport was small and reflected the state of the Cuban economy. Mark noticed that the airport employees resembled a casting call for the next "Bond Girl." We wondered if Cuba wanted to make a good impression.

As we waited for our bags, I noticed the carousel was loaded with flat screen TVs, still boxed. I had never seen that before. We were told flat screens aren't available for purchase in Cuba so they are commonly brought back by family from the U.S.

Walking out the back of the terminal to our right was the quintessential Cuban sight.

Several dozen American cars from the 1950s, all makes and models, waited as taxis for foreign visitors. Cuba is often spoken of as a "time warp," and this certainly gave us that impression.

As our bus wove through Havana, history became the present. Billboards from the Cuban Revolution in 1959 stood out. Proud but badly faded, they showed the likeness of a young Fidel Castro. Slogans, in Spanish, reminded the Cuban people "We Must Be United!"

We stayed at the Hotel Nacional—a once opulent, still distinguished, place. Castro had stayed there during the most difficult moments of the Cuban Missile Crisis during the JFK presidency. The impressive, well-manicured back patio of the hotel overlooks Havana Bay and the boardwalk called the Malecon.

This trip was part of the "people-to-people program" with an itinerary centered on the arts. We were an audience to an incredible women's choir and an interpretive dance group that reminded me of the lady from the gym.

We visited a city block that the residents had converted into a walk-through art exhibit. The artists resourcefulness, in lieu of legitimate supplies, was admirable. The ACIS tour leaders deftly consolidated a three-day itinerary into two days. Nothing was missed.

The only true restaurant we visited was the iconic "Sloppy Joes." We were told it pre-dated the revolution. Dinner Saturday and lunch Sunday were eaten at "Paladares" which are government approved (of course) restaurants within a family home. The food was outstanding at both Paladares. Seafood options were popular as was the beef and pork. All wonderfully prepared.

Saturday night, our first night, was jam packed with dinner and the aforementioned choir. Afterward we sat on the incredible patio for hours. A day that started with a 4:45am wake-up call ended at about 1:30am. The lack of sleep has yet to show any ill-effects.

Sunday morning, I went onto that patio to workout. There was a cannon aimed at the harbor from the Spanish-American War of 1898. Another area advertised a locked entrance to a military trench line built in the 1960s. Knowing the history of these events, it was a great place for an old-school Rocky Balboa workout—sets of push-ups and lunges until the body screamed.

I got into the workout under a bright sun on a perfect 65-degree morning. A short time later, I looked off to my left and saw clouds and a rainbow. Above me were clear skies. I thought it odd there was a rainbow with no rain. Nine out of ten chimps at a zoo would have known *it is raining over there*! Occasionally I am shocked by my own stupidity.

Before I knew it, I was getting absolutely pounded by a storm. *Completely* soaked, I started to run for cover before stopping and thinking, "*Why? Would running keep me dry?*" I also realized, during my walk of shame back to the hotel entrance, the people looking at me were the ones doing the "people watching." Deservedly, I was the butt of the joke.

Late morning Sunday allowed for a few hours of a walking tour in *Old Havana*. Excellent old-world architecture dominated the area. Some buildings and blocks have gotten funding from UNESCO to be restored and preserved. Most of the area languishes, thirsty for power washing and fresh paint.

Business was about to pick up.

Late in the walking tour, we were taken to a store that sold high-quality rum, cigars and coffee. Unfortunately, the store was far smaller than the group, and it felt like a clown car experiment.

Mark said he was going elsewhere. Some men outside had promised better deals at their store, which they said was *right next door*. He walked out of the store and his past travel incidents flashed through my mind. He has been chased by bad guys in Bethlehem and once had to scramble to a tour bus to avoid a stampeding wild camel in Egypt.

I figured I better follow.

The store wasn't *right next door*. Mark was about half a football field in front of me, and after we walked a couple of blocks, I noticed the two salesmen originally escorting us had morphed into five. I started to think we were in some trouble. A Cuban man beside me pitched products in Spanglish at auctioneer speed, despite my telling him I wasn't buying anything.

We were led toward a ramshackle, abandoned building. It looked like it had barely survived a bombing. I seriously questioned if the staircase leading up would hold my 200lbs. Up one flight, a room had a folding table and some cigars to purchase.

Amazingly, the man next to me was still pitching things that I had told him 700 times I wouldn't buy. Mark was trying to buy two cigars while they were trying to sell him 100. It looked sketchy.

The "dude" in me had already considered the odds. Five of them vs two of us.

Mark and I were far bigger than all of them but Cuba has compulsory military service. They all had military training.

Yet another man was standing in the doorway. Was he blocking it, or just standing there? I was unsure if this was a sale or a mugging and I'd rather know that answer than to meekly find out the hard way, so I walked right toward him and said, "Excuse me." This may have been a bold, or stupid, decision considering the odds against us. However, the guy in the door had the build of a compulsive "gamer," who sees sunlight as often as a vampire, and walks around with potato chip crumbs on his shirt,

As I neared him, he stepped aside, relieving some tensions. Mark bought two cigars and we headed out of the rubble. The Cuban men immediately veered in another direction. "Dude, what were you thinking???" I asked. Mark laughed and acknowledged that trusting them wasn't the best idea.

We rejoined our group and several people expressed concern about what happened. The owner of the store we had left yelled at those men as we were led away. It appeared they were as unsavory as we suspected.

ACIS had planned a farewell party at the Havana Beach Club on Sunday night. It was a place built by a gangster in the pre-revolution days. He was later "out-gangstered" by Castro and the communists. He coughed up the beach club and left Cuba for good.

Having taken tour buses everywhere thus far, we were lead to over 20 of the old American cars awaiting as our taxis—a classy gesture on ACIS behalf. We claimed a pink Cadillac whose driver was a young guy—friendly—but spoke little English. The "time warp taxis" caravanned through Havana. These cars were 100% original. In no way had they been customized due to financial and supply constraints.

Sixty-year-old windshields are kind of opaque; you can't see through them clearly. Factor in the darkness, and the front seat of a convertible may not have been the place to be. The car in front of us spewed heavy exhaust from its antique engine, blurring the windshield further.

At red lights, our driver would wipe the inside of the windshield with a rag. I noticed no improvement. Tempted to mention the exhaust was on the *outside* of the windshield, I clammed up to avoid being the know-it-all American. I wondered how effective a 60-year-old seat belt would be.

The Havana Beach Club had once been the "it" place. Now a bit outdated but still regal, the party was great. At one point, I stood in the sand at water's edge. It was *very* windy and uncomfortably chilly. A man from our group sidled up and told me the beach club sat on the very spot upon which Columbus had landed in Cuba.

My love of history was piqued, but the source was dubious. The man seemed intelligent but was incredibly drunk. I was not sure if he was speaking to me or the palm tree.

We arrived back at the Nacional close to 11pm. Knowing our last hours in Cuba were near, we found a bar a few blocks away called "The One-Eyed Cat." A band played and was very good.

It closed at 3am, and we walked back to the hotels. We hung in the lobby of one hotel chatting with people from the group. I got back to my room just before sunrise. By 10am, Havana was in the rear-view mirror. By 11pm on Monday, I was in my own bed.

I walked into my classroom Tuesday morning, enjoying the last bit of silence I would have that day. It sunk in that 24 hours earlier I awoke in Cuba, had lunch in Miami and slept in St. Louis. Despite the whirlwind, my daily routine had been restored as though the entire weekend had been an overnight dream.

I marveled at how the complete lack of sleep never bothered me. The adrenaline of a great trip at a sad time in my personal life had negated it. The bell rang and the sixth graders poured in with an energy unique to them.

They knew of my trip and wanted to hear about it. Needing to move on to that day's history lesson, I told them it had been a phenomenal two days in Cuba. One of the girls, mature beyond her age, said, "I thought you were going for three days?"

"So did we," I replied. "Okay, here is what happened." My 11 and 12-year-old students left that day having learned a lesson in patience and making the best of a bad situation. And learned that luggage can be held hostage—something I didn't know a week earlier.

Most of the time, trips are pre-planned well ahead of time. The well-known touristy spots book up well in advance which makes shuffling events around difficult. Though the trip was shortened, and the entire itinerary rearranged, we still did everything we were scheduled to do.

Once in a while though, you bump into an opportunity you never knew about—a dive restaurant with fantastic food or a road trip like the one we discovered on the next trip to Banff in Alberta, Canada.

CHAPTER 5 - CANADA

In the summer of 2016, I journeyed up to the Canadian Rockies to visit the mountain town of Banff. I was traveling with my friend Mark, who also cohosts my travel podcast Peanut Butter and Passports, along with my cousin Dave. Both of them are educated, sports-loving chaps with loads of international travel experience. They treat people well and are good to travel with. It promised to be a week of predictable male behavior, alternating between hiking and feasting in restaurants.

I had heard of Banff in numerous ways. It seems to appear on every list of quaint mountain towns. Filter the list to "Great Places to Visit in Canada," and you will find Banff featured there as well. Being a lover of mountain towns, it had been on my "list" for years.

Banff is a small town most easily accessed by flying into Calgary, about 90 minutes away. In the province of Alberta, both Calgary and Banff celebrate their Western heritage much like people in the western states of the U.S. We arrived in cowboy country, nothing more than city slickers whose list of country boy skills could fit in a fortune cookie.

At the airport, all of the employees were wearing brown cowboy hats and uniforms with western leanings. Extraordinarily friendly and welcoming, they demonstrated the region's history and western culture to everyone that arrived.

The famed Calgary Stampede Rodeo took place while we were there. Billboards and signage everywhere advertised the event. In hindsight, I wish we had attended. Rodeo is *f-a-r* outside of my experiences. My becoming a rodeo star was less likely than an entire boy band becoming Tibetan monks.

The fact cowboys and I have nothing in common is a negative comment toward me, not them. There is no more rugged civilian dude than the cowboy working 12-hour days on a ranch in all weather. I have crazy respect for them; it's a proud but difficult life.

When traveling to cowboy country you are walking in ground inhabited by very tough and disciplined people. A lot of men think of themselves as rugged and tough, the Cro-Magnon version of "manly." Many have clearly earned the title of "manly" in various ways; others simply want to be seen that way. I am sure there is another group of males that truly doesn't care how they are classified. Cowboys are near the top of the list in traditional "manly" qualities. Only soldiers may rank higher.

There is no group more noble than soldiers—they are the definition of "bravery and toughness." Perhaps that is a reason there are far more movies about Navy SEALS than accountants and teachers.

The civilian version of soldier is likely thought to be police officers and firefighters who, admirably, face personal danger in an attempt to keep others safe.

Far away from the mainstream, rodeo cowboys perform before tiny crowds, huge ones and even on TV. They can make big money, but at the definite risk of gruesome injury. Not as noble, or revered, as soldiers, the rodeo cowboys still have respect heaped upon them.

Visitors to the Louvre in Paris, at some point, may wonder what life would be like if they had artistic talents. Similarly, arriving to a western town made me appreciate the quiet toughness and pride that cowboys are known for.

Choosing to sit on the back of a huge, powerful bull, which is highly motivated to throw you off and gore you repeatedly is an interesting career choice. There are docile animals willing to let humans hitch rides on their backs.

Bulls aren't among them.

Typically, the mere presence of the rider, and his weight, is ample reason for a bull to buck. That alone isn't enough for competitive bull riding. To further agitate the bull, a "flank strap" is tightened around the area of the animal's nether regions. Whether or not the strap causes pain, or merely pressure, depends upon who you hear it from. The bull is rarely asked.

Many involved in the rodeo circuit defend the sport to detractors who think the sport is unfair to animals. They say there is no pain, just pressure. I am not sure there is much difference. Pressure on the "nether regions" can only be highly unpleasant. If someone tightened a strap around my plumbing, I would be bucking, kicking and trying to hurt someone as well.

Nearly any other occupation these cowboys could have chosen would be far easier and immeasurably safer. That's why I admire them. Riding the furious bull, feeling its strength and anger, has to be a fear-soaked adrenaline rush. The cowboys get flung forward and backward like rag dolls as the bull kicks. The rider's arms and head flailing about due to the bulls powerful thrashing would likely cause my head to snap off like a Lego.

I'm not sure I would even choose to be a rodeo clown—the hero who intentionally distracts the bull, draws his wrath and runs for the hills while the fallen cowboy is attended to. It's so counterintuitive to intentionally draw the ire of the raging bull toward you when instinct says to run in the opposite direction.

One reason I will never go to Pamplona, Spain, to watch the "running of the bulls" is the likelihood I would make history. The bulls would disregard the people running from them and somehow magnetically target me in the crowd watching. The people standing in front of me would part like the Red Sea, ignored as the angry Bull chose me. "Man screams" would be heard as I was tossed about and stomped on before being skewered with its horns.

In that way, I am uniquely qualified to be a rodeo clown. I could attract their attention without trying.

In previous trips to Cuba, Peru and Bolivia there was a certain adrenaline buzz connected to spending time in a place where you don't speak the language.

Of course, I mastered the most important phrase one needs in a Spanish-speaking country: "Donde esta el bano?" Where is the bathroom?

I can only imagine the physical comedy for others to see if I had an urgent bathroom emergency, like in Hawaii, without even knowing what sign to look for. One would observe me waddling around like a penguin, in a "full panic sweat," pirouetting like a ballerina searching for any sign showing a toilet.

Traveling to Canada, an English-speaking country, removed all of those problems. Or most of them. One doesn't prepare for language barriers in a country that speaks the same language as you do.

One should.

A foreigner visiting the United States may wonder how all of these crazy Americans can communicate with each other. Bostonians with the famous "Baaah-ston" dialect may struggle to respond to a Mississippian greeting them with a slow, "Hoowww. Yyyaaawwwlll doooiiinnn?"

While fast talking New Yorkers say "pahk" instead of "park" as though the letter "r" doesn't exist, a California valley girl frustratingly uses the word "like" about six times per sentence.

The bigger the country, the more varied the dialects of that language. I doubt the Mediterranean island nation of Malta has a great range of dialects. Lichtenstein, a country so small a golden retriever could pee on all of its borders in a single day, likely doesn't either.

Canada is a big country, and multi-lingual. I had no idea French had as much presence in Western Canada as it does. With English being the prevalent language in Alberta, we met no Canadians that spoke only French. Assuming French was quarantined into Quebec province may have been naïve—it was certainly wrong.

Much like businesses in the U.S. are making life easier for Spanish speakers—providing Spanish options at ATMs and on signage in stores—the grocery store we went to provided the same courtesy towards their French speaking countrymen.

Having not researched this prior to the trip, the visit to the store was surprising and reminded me how much I don't know—a list that certainly would not fit on a Post-it note.

We arrived in Banff and checked into our condo, about a mile from downtown. This wasn't just a mile in length; it was a steep hill. Checking in, we were greeted by two young ladies, one British and the other an Aussie. Both were working in Banff as part of the "working holiday," or "gap year" program the countries in the British Commonwealth take part in.

I love this program. These workers are usually just out of high school or slightly older. They gain life experience living abroad and working, typically in the service industry. It is a great head start to becoming a well-rounded, worldly and educated person in my view.

Later in the week, I spoke with a lady in a coffee shop. She was originally from Australia and came to Banff as part of the same program. She came with a group of friends, 25 years earlier. She was so taken by Banff she chose to stay. Another from that group lives in Calgary while the rest eventually made their way back down under.

She told me they took their kids back to Australia to meet family and friends they always heard about. Though Banff is breathtakingly easy on the eyes in the summer, it likely gets no warmer than jacket weather. Australia is quite the opposite.

They traveled there and stayed for a year, happy to provide their kids that life experience. They also wanted their children to see Australia as a viable place to attend college if they preferred. She said the kids really enjoyed the year spent there, were impressed, but were very glad to get home to Banff when they did.

Sun and beaches "do it" for many people. There is always that hearty group that enjoys the cool-to-cold climates. After spending time in a "snow globe" town surrounded by mountains at all times, it's easy to understand why.

I am completely entranced by mountain towns. My choice of where to live, however, is overridden by my hatred of shoveling snow, shivering and being tempted to put on a gorilla mask to save my ears from frostbite.

In the summer, there is no better place to be. Banff is an interesting place in that it is technically a park, not a town. In Canada, people can live in national parks. Most of Banff National Park's land is raw, rugged nature with no development. The towns near those open spaces are also part of the parks.

One of the complications with living in a national park is the fact homeowners don't own the land the house sits on. They sign leases that last many decades and function the same as owning the land title as well. Yet some people are leery the government will abuse that situation.

About 30 minutes from Banff is a nice town called Canmore. Locals told me many people prefer to live there. Not being the hub of tourism, things are cheaper and less congested. Canmore also sits outside the boundaries of Banff National Park, allowing home-owners to buy the land.

On our first day, we walked the area to get our bearings and enjoy the views. Alpine settings are my favorite. Downtown Banff only has a few roads cutting through it. There are, of course, restaurants, cafés and enough tourist shops to hold the entire population of Luxembourg, it seemed.

Walking just a mile outside of town, you are in a truly rugged area. Walking alongside major roads that intersect highways, there are still signs warning of bears, wolves and elk. The Canadian Rockies mean business.

We enjoyed thick steaks, then began our walk back up the hill to the condo. Some hills really test a person's stamina while others test your patience. This was truly a steep uphill, one mile in length and was about to test our ability to simply pay attention.

Though we would laugh about this days later, having just arrived nothing looked familiar. It was basically a long ribbon of pavement, framed by guardrails, surrounded by mountains and evergreens.

We came to a fork in the road and chose left with no hesitation. Not far past it, the three of us wondered if we were going the right direction. It all looked the same. Being guys, we joked about all of the things that could go wrong but left it "at the joke level." Inside, we probably were all more concerned then we let on.

Sadly people disappear every year while camping or hiking in the wilderness. Often, their body or remains are found months or years later. Sometimes they are never found at all. Not by humans anyway. This situation was not yet dangerous but couldn't be laughed off either.

We continued walking with no confidence, fully aware the sun was setting. Plummeting with the sun would be the temperatures. As night arrives and people tend to slow down, many four-legged predators are just stretching their legs to begin looking for dinner.

Eventually a unanimous vote sent us back to the fork and in the other direction. Thankfully so. It led us to the condo where we could sit and scheme the plans for the next several days.

The trip was off to a great start, but could very easily have ended poorly. It made me realize how often a simple mistake, or refusal to correct it, can have unfortunate or tragic consequences.

I can eat. I mean *really* eat. I am also a health fanatic and that is a strange duality I fight daily. In some respects, they go together well. Working out hard requires a lot of caloric intake—the inverse is true as well.

I am fortunate to love foods that many hate. Broccoli is my "little green compadre." Steamed and seasoned properly, I can enjoy broccoli with any meal, partially because I know the favor I just did for my body. Quinoa, salmon, chia seeds, acai berries and all of the other "super foods" are friends of mine as well.

Then there is my dietary dark side. Having already mentioned my legendary sweet tooth, I admit to routinely eating entire large pizzas or platters of nachos. The alert my brain is supposed to receive to indicate "being full" is apparently broken.

There have been times when dining gluttony leaves me lying down and sweating two hours later. Meals that Paul Bunyan could not choke down cause me little discomfort most of the time, so working out is a daily must.

The "main event" of our trip was going to be a visit to the legendary Lake Louise to see for ourselves if the water could actually be that funky, electric, exotic shade of blue.

We planned that day in synch with the weather forecast. The week of our stay had a literal dark cloud hanging over it, according to meteorologists. Clouds and rain were predicted for every day but one. Naturally, we enjoyed mostly great weather.

The original game plan, arrived at the night before, was to make that day trip a few days later, on what looked like the only great weather day we would get.

Knowing that we would be eating like savages for a week, I had planned a workout regimen. The only equipment I needed was a park bench and space. Given such, I could start each day with a great "body weight" workout to offset the caloric monkey business that was sure to follow.

I gathered some things, headed down the hill and arrived downtown about 7am. It was chilly but fortunately still dry with no wind.

There was a park, smaller than a billionaire's walk-in closet, just off of the sidewalk lining the main drag through town. I began a workout with the intention of doing sets of lunges and push-ups.

The plan was to do 10 sets of 30 each, with 20 seconds rest in between sets. Energized by the start of a vacation, the early and middle sets went better than usual, though the last few sets were grueling due to the short rest interval, the elevation and—well—the fact I was 48.

After finishing, I set a new goal, my highest total ever, so it would definitely be challenging. The rest of the day planned to be low-key and casual so killing it in a workout made a lot of sense. I added 200 more of each, also divided into 10 sets.

I hammered through a very difficult final stretch, with the help of songs from the Rocky soundtrack. Those inspiring tunes allowed me to mentally "BE" young and chiseled, temporarily forgetting that at 48, I was neither. There is always a mirror to eventually remind you that Father Time is undefeated.

The twenty seconds of recovery became several minutes between sets.

Then it became two songs in between.

The last couple of sets were of the straining variety. Face red, arms quivering and involuntarily grunting, my final four push-ups seemed to last a minute apiece.

Push-ups do not provide much of a view, unless seeing the ground advancing and retreating is what you're looking for. Yet, I noticed there were four feet standing to my right, toes pointed at me. Finishing my last push-up, I stood up only long enough to take a seat on the bench.

The owners of those four feet came over to me. They belonged to an older Asian couple that, in my presence, spoke no English. We gestured for a couple of minutes, while he continued to speak to me as though I understood him. I must have been nodding convincingly. Eventually it was clear they wanted a picture with me.

I was perplexed, and immediately assumed they mistook me for someone famous. Not sure who, I wanted to think Brad Pitt or Ryan Reynolds, but feared they may think I looked like Yoda or a tall, red-faced Hobbit or maybe Bigfoot with a bad case of mange.

We took the pictures on her phone, and they walked off after nodding. He continued to talk the entire time. I would love to have a written transcript of whatever he was saying. I wondered what will they tell people when they show them that picture. I, immediately after a workout, face as red as a baboon's caboose, will be giggled at by countless strangers.

If they thought I was a celeb, at least the photo made sense. If not, is it just another of many completely random pictures they collect? What other things do they take pictures of? "Look Honey, toilet paper! Get a picture." "Dear, look at the trash can. Let's get a picture." "Babe, check out those pepper shakers. We need a picture." "Sweetie, look! Someone dropped a straw. Let's get a picture." And so it goes.

Finished with the workout, and potentially soon to be famous somewhere in Asia, I headed across the street to Evelyn's Coffee Shop.

Enjoying coffee and a breakfast sandwich while reading news on my laptop, I noticed twitching in my right thigh. It didn't hurt; in fact, the workout left me pleasantly exhausted. The twitching was "proof of progress," as I like to think of it—evidence of a great workout.

One of the benefits of working out is the metabolism in over-drive to gobble calories like a Pac-Man afterward. This would be a day of "after-burn"—casually enjoying the day, while the workout provided benefits long afterward. Or so I thought.

After a moment spent celebrating the workout, I got a text. Mark and Dave had made the executive decision that a change in plans was necessary. Now at about 9am, skies were clear and temperatures pleasant. What better day to go hiking around Lake Louise.

I couldn't disagree.

Not sure what lay ahead from a difficulty standpoint, there was no reason to mention the depth of the morning workout to the guys. Pre-emptive explanations of potential failure aren't my style. There is always time for that in my eulogy if I overdo it to the extreme.

I gathered my stuff and headed up the one-mile 'hill of death." Having already grinded through a work out that morning, one that left my thighs twitching, this was going to be a legitimate day of "shut up and hike."

And there would be food at the end.

Despite Banff actually being in a national park, it looks like a town. Arrival at Lake Louise actually felt like arriving at a distinguished park. One thing I never mind opening my wallet for is entrance into national parks.

Gandhi once was quoted as saying, "The greatness of a nation and its moral progress can be judged by the way its animals are treated. I'll hold that the more helpless a creature, the more entitled it is to protection by man from the cruelty of humankind."

Not only do I agree with that quote verbatim, I would happily apply the sentiment to "public lands." Canada values the gifts with which it has been bestowed.

The Fairmount Chateau Lake Louise is an upscale hotel perched on edge of the majestic lake. Though there are *some* rooms with small balconies facing the lake, I was surprised by how few. To wake up and sit on the balcony looking down on that lake is bucket list worthy—especially if your thighs aren't twitching.

The park also has an expansive patio designed for guests, whether they are staying at the hotel or not. Visiting there in July, tourists buzzed the entire area, many carrying the dreaded selfie stick.

It's hard to understand how civilization thrived and mankind was able to build and innovate so many things for centuries without the ability to take a selfie. Now it is an epidemic gone crazy.

To avoid tourists, one only has to seek out the hardest hiking trails. I'm willing to theorize that the most ambitious hikers, those willing to hurt and struggle bit, are rarely the ones indulging in the craze of the selfie stick.

To escape the glut of people, and avoid the risk of being bashed in the skull by an errant selfie stick, we headed upwards.

Lake Louise is surrounded by a network of trails that cross one another at some point.

Heading uphill, the crowds were quickly left down below. A perfect number of hikers traipsed up over 1000 vertical feet from lakeside. This hike was a "thigh burner" that cranked the calves pretty good as well. It was a challenge.

During the hike, one can see glimpses of the fabulous blue water below.

Tree trunks framed the lake from dozens of angles and views. Pictures of Lake Louise are one of the most common things seen when searching for beautiful nature photos. It truly looks photo-shopped.

A sign along the way explained the strange blue is created by minerals unique to that area. Shots of the blue water through the brown of tree trunks and green of pine needles were really hard to believe.

As we hiked, the smell of evergreens was notable. The dense forest was well-shaded with a perfect amount of light leaking through. Twigs occasionally snapped underfoot—a phenomenal alpine hike.

Throughout the day, chipmunks were skittering here and there, and I was struck by their size. This area just may have the largest chipmunks on earth. They seem to have a good gig. The weather and elevation may eliminate snakes from their list of concerns. The density of the trees would make "death from above" in the talons of many birds of prey unlikely as well. Owls may be their only menace.

If a person were to get injured while hiking in the area, they could be dragged off thrashing and screaming by four mega-chipmunks while they waited for help to arrive.

That's humiliation.

"Man Succumbs to a Chipmunk Attack" is not the headline you want circulated through Facebook to update friends on your cause of death. Here, I wouldn't rule it out.

We hiked for hours, totaling over 10 miles and dozens of chipmunks. Meeting people along the way and having some nice conversations reaffirmed what I love about traveling.

We arrived in Banff for a mid-evening dinner after cleaning up. A restaurant, The Bear St. Tavern, came highly recommended and we wound up eating there again on the trip. That night, with complete full body exhaustion, there would be no thought given to broccoli, asparagus and the like. It was a pizza night. The Big Bird pizza, co-starring chicken and bacon, was excellent. The pie, combined with local ciders, made for an optimal reward for a tough day on the body.

When traveling, it is often inspiring to meet people and simply learn how they are living their lives. Though cliché', the saying "You are the star of your own life story" always bounces around my head, and our waitress exemplified that. She explained that she and her husband live in Banff part of the year and in the Netherlands the rest of the time.

They have managed to carve out a life living in two places they adore. We didn't get into the details of how they make it work, but I so admired their willingness to live an unconventional life if that's what they desired. On their last day alive, they likely won't have any regrets. Rather, they may inspire people along the way, nudging them closer to something they have always wanted to do.

One day was so rainy, we capitulated and looked for indoor entertainment. Our condo was both modest and small. "Stir Crazy" is no way to spend a vacation. I was browsing the web for ideas and saw a National Geographic list of Great Drives in the World. One of them started in Banff.

This changed the day dramatically. Driving from Banff National Park to another town/park combo called

Jasper National Park was described by National Geographic as "one of the crown jewels of western Canada." We were in!

The road trip would take a full day, with each leg of it about four hours long. I've been fortunate to drive some incredible stretches in the world, none better than this. The Death Road in Bolivia was outstanding, if the possibility of imminent death doesn't dissuade you.

The Ring of Kerry in Ireland showed the complete spectrum of every shade of green, enhanced by bright sunshine and shade from clouds. The hilly terrain provided crazy undulations that made the drive seemingly unbeatable.

The ride from Queenstown, New Zealand, to the edge of the South Island to tour Milford Sound was eye-poppingly impressive. An array of bold colors contrasted with the charming site of more sheep then I knew even existed.

Both of those drives feature hills and low mountains. For more majestic peaks, the "Million Dollar Highway," U.S. route 550 in southwestern Colorado, left me gape-jawed and drooling. It is truly spectacular. The Pacific Coast Highway in California is an epic drive as well.

Two very underrated drives from my experience are both worthy of mention. Highway 285 in Colorado, which leads from the southern Denver metro area to the mountain resorts near Breckenridge, is 90 minutes of "Wow!"

One day, driving through there with my sister, we happened upon some "Pasture Action"—two horses in a very amorous moment. They could not have been closer to the road if they tried. A fence kept them from wandering onto the road, but unfortunately it was the type of fence that hid nothing from sight. The pasture land is so expansive it was incredibly unlikely these two horses would carry on like lovers on a nude beach *right by the road*. It seemed like a laugh sent to us as a gift. My sister and I cackled until we cried and then giggled sporadically the rest of the drive.

Thankfully, Highway 285 has very, very low traffic volume most days—the only thing preventing a massive, multi-car pileup had just one driver glanced over at these two horses in love.

The Beartooth Highway connects southwestern Montana with Yellowstone Park in Wyoming. I was stunned by the surreal site as I entered Montana. A fast-moving river ran alongside the road, dancing from the left side, to the right, and back again in the serpentine fashion that rivers have. With fly fisherman standing in the torrent, and with mountains standing guard, this setting was postcard worthy.

All of those drives are spectacular yet none of them are better than Highway 93, connecting Banff and Jasper. The drive was like a conveyor belt that continually brought amazing views—mountains, evergreen forests, lakes and rivers in a colorful array that would leave one speechless.

On both legs of the trip, traffic stopped as a bear ambled across the road. Jasper is nearly due north of Banff. A four-hour drive north of anything in Canada can land you in pretty raw territory. Fortunately, it was a very pleasant day in Jasper when we arrived. Also a small town, Jasper reminded me more of Canmore than Banff. They both are a little more linear and spread out compared to Banff's compact, grid-like downtown area.

It was a quaint town with some charm. We walked around finding a spot for lunch before heading back south. Between the two cities was an opportunity we couldn't pass up.

The Columbia Icefield area has guided tours out onto the Athabasca Glacier. Taking a "glacier walk" was something I had never considered, or even knew was possible. To get from the visitor center to the icefields, we were loaded into buses different from anything I had seen before. Your mental image of a yellow school bus should be thrown out. This looked like a small bus sitting on top of a monster truck.

The tires were enormous. The deep treads made navigating deep snow possible, while the massive width of the tire made it less likely to break through the ice.

As we arrived, the bus paused at the top of an extraordinarily steep hill. I'm not sure I've ever driven down a hill this steep. It is exactly the type of hill every teenage boy wishes they could go sledding down, and precisely the type of hill that keeps emergency rooms busier than they would like.

To navigate this hill, the bus had six axles, with each axle controlled by its own transmission. I know absolutely nothing about cars. My automotive knowledge base includes how to pump gas, change tires and call for help, but I know that one transmission per vehicle is standard.

I was surprised how slowly the bus was able to go down the hill. The multiple transmissions were in play for this very reason. We tipped downward only moving two or three miles an hour. It was impressive that a vehicle of such weight could descend a hill at the pace of a box turtle.

Reaching the flat area at the bottom of the hill, we could notice this area had clearly been prepared for visitors. A large flat circle allowed the bus room to maneuver. The circle was created each morning by the crew in advance of tourists. They had special equipment to tamp down and strengthen that area, making it relatively safe for vehicles and people.

Beyond that circle consisted of jagged ice features and outcroppings. The glacier itself had the texture and topography of an unmade bed, certainly not flat and smooth, it was a large slab of ice sliding through a gap in mountains.

We were told not to walk off of the flattened area. Cautionary tales were told of people who had wandered outside of the prepared area, only to step into hidden crevasses, usually with gruesome results. Some glaciers have seracs, which are towers of ice which can collapse suddenly, smashing or maiming any tourist underneath.

The guide spoke of a tourist who broke through the ice to a shallow crevasse. An undercurrent of water below the glacier swept him forward and spit him out at the front edge of the glacier. Battered, bruised and freezing, the bewildered dude got off relatively unscathed.

There were places where one could look straight down and see water flowing below the ice. We were at a far higher elevation at the Columbia Icefields. Banff sits just 4,000 feet (1300m) above sea level and Jasper is lower at just over 3,000 feet (1,000m). Between the two, elevations climb dramatically. The Athabasca Glacier rests between 10,000 and 13,000 feet (3,000-4,000m), so the pleasant temperatures in the towns were now uncomfortably cold after just a few minutes on the glacier.

The guide was able to point toward the visitor center we had just left. It was nearly a mile (1.6 kilometers) away. It served as a perfect reference point for how far the glacier had receded. Many decades ago, the glacier extended all the way from where we were standing to where the visitor center is now.

Most of the guides and bus drivers come from all over Canada. Ours was from the province of Manitoba and had come to western Canada seeking better employment opportunities. Many of them had migrated from other places as well.

They were all young, a mixture of men and women. He pointed out a building where they all stayed. The glacier and icefields are largely in the middle of nowhere. The employees have very limited options for housing, dining etc. Each of the employees I encountered was outgoing and friendly, as guides need to be.

They also had a bit of a wild streak. I had the distinct feeling there were crazy times in the communal housing they lived in—kind of like the pasture along highway 285 in Colorado

Dave and I went on a hike not far from Banff. Per custom, the lower area closest to the parking lot was buzzing with tourists. The spot had numerous waterfalls and was really very pleasant. The walkways down low were paved, making it much more of a walk than a hike.

That lends this place to being very popular with the less mobile and those not looking for a workout. All of that blended together meant moving around was slow and tedious, so we headed uphill.

Parts of this were very steep but with solid footing and no real danger. As is common in hiking, people you pass at some points end up passing you. A leapfrog of sorts, all caused by different paces and break times.

Dave and I are your classic middle-aged guys who keep in good shape, have never been compelled to get ink or piercings, and generally look non-threatening. As we journeyed upward, we came upon two ladies we had seen several times already.

These ladies had pulled over to nosh on some snacks they made. As we wandered up alongside them they extended the food and said, "Want some snacks?" Male psychology is really quite simple; offer guys food and they will accept. We gobbled a variety of things they had.

Being clean-cut and nonthreatening doesn't make us smart. These ladies fit the same description as we did, and we certainly had no concerns eating what they gave us.

We laughed later about how quickly we ate things offered by total strangers. We would be the perfect marks for people with any type of dubious motives who were smart enough to offer us food.

Pet owners can often induce their cat or dog to give up a toy, spot on the couch or anything else the owner wants by simply offering them a treat. The dog, for example, will hop down and run over to snarf the treat, completely unaware they have been manipulated with food. Apparently, I work the same way. Keep feeding me cookies and I will follow you anywhere.

Snacks laced with drugs would have left us staggering through a forest and possibly chewing on trees like enthusiastic beavers. We read these ladies correctly, they were trustworthy in every way. It was still likely a bad decision to take food from people you haven't even said "hello" to yet.

These ladies lived in Calgary and were longtime friends. We hiked together for a few hours, enjoying a fun and casual conversation.

Eventually signs indicated we had reached the end of the trail system, yet the trail visibly extended beyond the signs, so we hiked onward. Laughing and talking as we walked, we saw another sign that warned of this being "bear country" and advised against hiking farther.

I don't need that explained any more simply. Translation: turn around and go back or else.

The ladies assured us they've hiked here before and there was nothing to worry about. That brought us to an interesting decision. The sign clearly showed there *is* danger. These friendly, active locals said there is *no* danger—they do it all time.

The same thing surfers say about sharks.

Sometimes in life, you just have to view things through the simplest prism possible. One way to do that is to ask yourself the question, "How will I look back on this if something goes wrong?" If one has a car wreck that was unforeseeable, and just bad luck, you can't regret the *decision* to make that drive.

If signs, social media and newspapers warn swimmers to stay out of the ocean because of shark sightings, a surfer who persists and loses a leg to a shark will likely realize his life was changed forever by bad decisions, not bad luck.

Faced with both warnings, and assurances, the smart thing to do would have clearly been to head back from where we came.

We headed farther into bear country.

The trail being so lightly used, it was very narrow, forcing us to hike single file. I chose to lead, figuring if we came upon bears, at least the other three people could run while I was swatted about, munched and chewed to oblivion by a grizzly. It was interesting leading the hike in a bear's turf. I tried to picture several scenarios and how to deal with them in the event they arose.

Occasionally video surfaces of a house cat or small dog bolting out of a house toward bears invading their backyard.

The bear has every physical advantage and is looking for food. A snack runs right toward them in the form of a small beagle or hamster-sized Pomeranian, yet the fervor and aggressiveness of the tiny defender causes the typically fierce predators to turn and run.

If we were to run into bears, I wanted it to be one of *those* bears. We hiked onward for about 30 minutes before turning back to safer areas, with Dave leading. Similar to our first walk in Banff where we were confused and on the brink of getting lost at nightfall, this was another situation where we returned home from a trip with great pictures and memories only because of good fortune, not good decisions.

Our final night arrived and after a predictably huge dinner, we headed back and packed. Our flight left early the next morning and required us to leave Banff, for the 90-minute drive to Calgary, in the predawn darkness.

Anyone who has traveled extensively has run into absolutely maddening experiences with airlines. This was one of those.

A flight out of Calgary scheduled for the evening before was cancelled due to a plane malfunction. Our flight was now the first one that morning. Dave and I had checked in for our flights online the night previous to departure. Mark tried to, but couldn't, and had to do that at the airport upon arrival.

All of the passengers for both of those flights arrived to check in. Self-serve kiosks were not available. Knowing the flight from the previous night was canceled, the airline foolishly still provided only a single agent to work with hundreds of travelers.

After waiting in line for 30 minutes and moving about two steps, it was clear that either loads of travelers would be stranded or flights would be delayed. Well-justified grumbling spread quickly.

If 90% of irritated travelers keep their gripes to themselves, there are always the 10%, who are irritated by everything they deal with, that will wage a holy war with whomever will listen.

These are the type of people, wired for negativity and conflict, that would drop an F bomb between the words "Happy" and "Birthday" in outrage if a rabbit had the nerve to scamper across the road. Forced to slow down, they arrive at the party two seconds later then they hoped, and regale the other partygoers about the indignity of it all. The type of people that find the negative in any situation.

Plenty of those people were in line with us. Eventually, another agent arrived. Of the three of us, Mark made it to an agent first. I was second at the other agent. I actually boarded our flight at the time it was scheduled to leave and was one of the first aboard the plane.

As it filled up, Dave walked on and took his seat, across the aisle and about seven seats in front of me. Eventually, the plane was full and prepared for takeoff. Dave turned to me and mouthed, "Where's Mark?" A question I did not know the answer to.

I checked my phone to see a string of texts from Mark angrily bashing the airline. Due to his inability to be able to check in the night before, the airline cancelled Mark's flight and gave that seat to a traveler stranded from the flight cancelled the night before.

He was suitably enraged and the texts insulted the airline in very creative ways. Shutting my phone off, I was eager to land in Minneapolis and check on his status. As Dave and I walked through the terminal in Minneapolis, casually finding food before our connecting flight, more texts arrived in a flurry.

Dave and I only had a short connecting flight from Minneapolis to St. Louis remaining. Mark was rushed onto a flight that was literally about to leave. He didn't even know where it was going. The airline sent him on a trip to three cities that took nearly 24 hours to get him home.

He was very polite in his dealings with the airline and, despite pointing out it was their mistake that caused all of this, they only offered him a $100 voucher as an apology. In the travel world, that is akin to smashing into someone's car with yours, and offering them a Girl Scout cookie as compensation.

We felt bad for him, but couldn't help laughing. That's what guys do.

Most people's best memories of traveling involve great times and laughter with friends and family—funny stories, or things you saw, that are retold countless times. That is the point of it all. However, difficulties can arise suddenly, and there was no one laughing about a situation on a flight during my next trip to New Zealand four months later.

CHAPTER 6 - NEW ZEALAND

A few months after the Banff trip, I headed out on a two-week solo trip to New Zealand. I have always thought of the island country as a gem in the South Pacific. Australia, a neighbor and cultural cousin to New Zealand, seems to get more attention. Having not been to Australia yet, I am comfortable saying it's likely amazing as well. Two friends living there swear to it.

Every country has natural scenery that can be breathtaking. Hikes often provide the opportunity to witness those wonders. Any worthwhile hike takes you far from the urban drumbeat. Mother Nature's best work often lies alongside, or at the end of, a good hike.

Hiking may reveal fjords, canyons or mountain tops reflected in lakes. That, honestly, is why I travel. I love a weekend in a big city too. Each metropolis is a stunning work in mankind's portfolio. A few thousand years ago, humans were celebrating cave painting, fire and—well—standing upright (Walking without stepping on one's fingers is very under-appreciated).

To any of us, that's an absurdly long time ago. Compared to the time Earth has existed though, 35,000 years is the equivalent of a single pebble of sand on a beach

Despite being shorter, hairier and smelling like a zoo, our primitive predecessors started the technological climb. Soon Egyptians were building pyramids and Romans constructed aqueducts without construction equipment of any kind. Human capability resulted in the existence of skyscrapers, airplanes and atomic bombs. What humans are able to create is astounding, especially the progress made in the comparatively short time since 1800.

Natural wonders always top my list though.

We are often reminded that Mother Nature, like most mothers, is calling the shots. Every monument to the greatness of man can be squashed like a cockroach by a number of natural menaces.

Despite the tragedy inherent in hurricanes, tornados and the like, each can serve as a "reset" button for those of us who think we have problems. Wi-Fi down? Car won't start? Favorite person eliminated from a reality show? It is amazing the things we lose our minds over.

I am as easy going as you'll find yet my mood can turn sour in an instant when I have to call customer service. If the agents are located outside of English-speaking countries, or there is no phone support at all, frustration takes the wheel.

Neither of those options represents "service" to me.

I am always polite to them, explaining that they speak my language *w-a-y* better than I speak theirs. Soon, however, my head starts to hurt. As the conversation continues, I feel super human strength surging through me and my face distorts like someone who smashed their thumb with a hammer.

Only my built-in tactful side prevents me from raging like the fan in the upper deck of a stadium, who screams insults at the players, coaches and officials knowing they will never hear the words.

During the call, I feel like I am on a hidden camera show. I expect some celebrity talk show host to pick up the phone, thank me for being a good sport then promise me a prize to offset the damage done to my heart and brain.

If ever requiring legal punishment, a judge should sentence me to "30 days of customer service calls" for maximum punitive effect. Bailiffs would haul me out, insisting I let go of the judge's leg while I cried out, *"No! Not that! I'll do anything*!!!"

All because the phone call was answered in Mumbai and not Minneapolis. So yes, humans lose our equilibrium over relatively random and pointless things.

Hiking tends to calm the soul. Being amidst the best sites nature has to offer medicates a lot of the silly ills we all seem to have.

I have hiked all throughout the Rocky Mountains. Aware that nefarious meat-eaters like bears, mountain lions and wolves occupy the terrain, I am undeterred by that. Australia's critters collectively are a much bigger deterrent. Illogically, snakes bother me more than four-legged predators in the U.S. that could chase me down from a distance.

Visiting Australia tops many lists. I am eager to see it myself and will certainly do so soon. Hiking through Australia, however, is not in my plans. Bully for those that do, but I'll pass.

Australia has snakes so venomous you might die *before* they bite you. The collection of serpents Australia was gifted with includes some that are aggressive, fast moving and known for bad tempers—like a New York

City driver but with fangs and venom. A bad combo for the rest of us.

Shouldn't the aggressive, ill-tempered manner have been installed in sloths instead? There would certainly be fewer victims.

The three-toed sloth is famous for moving slowly. So slow, I am not sure video of them can be fast-forwarded. If a sloth were to "lash out" at you, you'd have about 30 minutes to duck or jump out of the way. They would hurt literally no one despite having formidable claws.

In the old black and white horror movies, victims were pursued by monsters such as mummies, or even Frankenstein. The monsters looked the part, but they couldn't run or even bend their knees. The worst athlete in gym class should have been able to trot ahead of them talking trash and never get caught. Who could a sloth possibly catch and maim?

Aggressive, fast moving snakes with bad tempers are bad. But there are worse.

Another Aussie serpent has venom that causes numbness, sweating and eventually breathing difficulties—the same physical response many "soon-to-be-fathers" get in the delivery room.

The Inland Taipan is known as the "fierce snake." No commentary needed.

Australia also has spiders seemingly the size of coyotes. The Huntsman Spider, though not venomous, is gnarly looking. Most U.S cities have venomous spiders, but they are the diameter of a coin. If a Huntsman were brought to the U.S., there would be mayhem—people screaming and sprinting out of their houses, abandoning their children, leaving all belongings behind.

Australia's waterways are no better. Lakes and ponds are full of crocodiles. Videos taken at night often show red eyes peering just above the water. I'd rather pet a Huntsman Spider than get near water there.

Australia's jellyfish may outnumber the population of Montana. An aircraft carrier, the U.S.S. Ronald Reagan, once drew so many jellyfish into its cooling system that repairs were needed.

Not to be upstaged, the shark community in the waters off Australia's coast is both large and ravenous. So many people get in the ocean there that the odds are incredibly low that any single person will get attacked. That's of no consolation to the sharks' actual victims.

Australia has wildlife that can kill you while you're in bed, sipping coffee or taking out the trash. New Zealand is the exact opposite. There are no land mammal predators in New Zealand bigger than a possum. None. No wolves, coyotes or bears. No badgers or big cats either.

New Zealand introduced rabbits a couple of centuries ago for the sport of hunting and as a food supply. Soon they had a rabbit epidemic. Who would have suspected rabbits multiplied so fast? To control the rabbit population, stoats were brought it. Stoats, like politicians, are members of the weasel family.

In the 1800s, New Zealand introduced possums. Australian possums to be clear.

Though Australia got the short end of the stick in the unfair world-wide distribution of things that can kill you, it at least got the "cute" possum. The American version is a vile fellow—kind of like an ugly mega-rat with piranha teeth.

In an embarrassing twist of policy, New Zealand is now trying to get rid of some of the mammal species *they brought in* due to their impact on the country's bird population. The Law of Unintended Consequences wins again.

If you were to be reincarnated as a sheep, horse or deer, you should pray you live in New Zealand. There is no risk of a bear, wolf or cougar attack. It's kind of frigid, but that beats having a leg bitten off. Those timid species haven't been told they are in the clear, or they simply choose not to believe. They still nervously glance around, checking for an attack that will never come.

Hikers in New Zealand reap that same benefit. Not only are the temperatures mild and the scenery beyond gorgeous, you'll never have to trip your friend and run to save yourself from a cougar attack.

Clint had been to New Zealand and raved about the South Island and encouraged me to spend the bulk of my time in that half of the country. And while I really enjoyed my week in Auckland, Clint proved to be right. The South Island is fabulous.

I spent a week on each island. Landing in Auckland, my first concern was simply moving around. The length of the flight from San Francisco is very distorted by time zones. In real time, it was about 13 hours.

Being bigger than the average guy, the window seat is not optimal. Though neither are middle, nor aisle seats. I got up in the middle of the overnight flight to visit the restroom once. That was my only chance to move around, aside from fidgeting.

There was Olympic-quality fidgeting happening. On the trip 12 years earlier to Peru, the awful back spasms made *not* moving around sound wonderful. Naturally, the lady beside me on that flight used the airplane bathroom so frequently I wondered if there was a cash giveaway inside.

On the flight to New Zealand, the body felt good. Wedged against the window, the two friendly people to my right managed to sleep seemingly the entire way.

The skinny aisle seven feet away that I could not get to, teased me. Imagine putting the Christmas tree and gifts in a locked room and allowing the children to only look at them through a window. Getting off of the plane sounded, and felt, fantastic.

After arriving in Auckland, I was on an airport shuttle, being dropped off at a Ramada hotel near the Sky Tower in the central business district. Two young guys from Colorado sat behind me, talking excitedly. They were headed to a hostel and planning their night. I had flashbacks to myself 25 years earlier. What kind of antics would a friend and I have gotten into on a trip like that? They told me they were heading to hike Australia a week later. I wonder if they survived the jellyfish swarms and tortoise-sized spiders.

The driver dropped me off at a regular stop and told me, "Just go that way one block and the hotel is on your left."

Several blocks later, I realized he was wrong. My phone was still groggy from the trip and of no help. I traipsed around Auckland looking like the ultimate tourist. I am all for exercise but prefer to do it without suitcases.

Experienced travelers will advise the less experienced to blend in with locals in foreign countries. Most Americans stand out for a variety of reasons. To start, we have an affection for hoodies that the rest of the world can't keep pace with. Baseball caps, college apparel, Crocs, Under Armour gear and cargo shorts scream *American!"*

If someone is traveling in, say, Israel, a guy wearing an Alabama hoodie is likely not from Tajikistan. Yes, that is a real place. Likewise, someone in Namibia wearing a Yankees cap is probably not from Saudi Arabia. It's pretty easy to narrow down.

The main benefit of blending in is to avoid the notice of the assorted "bad guys" that may be lurking.

If a country exists where a tourist can feel extremely safe, it is New Zealand. It is frequently ranked as one of the safest countries on Earth. I sensed they could have just one cop on duty at all times and things would be fine.

I discovered it is one of the friendliest countries as well. I was repeatedly impressed by the welcoming and trusting nature of the people which I'll assume is proof I don't look like a serial killer.

The biggest perk of traveling solo is total control of the daily itinerary. Finally arriving at the Ramada, I checked in and took a nap. Four hours later, I made the short walk to the waterfront searching for food and fun. Deciding not to ask for recommendations, nor use my phone, I walked with the hopes of discovering something interesting.

Auckland reminds me of San Diego, just with cooler weather. It has been ranked "Best City in the World," and I can see why. It has a sparkling marina, countless restaurants and cafés along with every amenity known to mankind. The Sky Tower is Auckland's signature piece—it's Gateway Arch or Space Needle. It stands many blocks from the water and atop higher ground.

Far higher.

Though its perch helps the directionally-challenged find their way, getting up there can elicit cursing in multiple languages if one is stubborn enough to walk.

While waiting to cross at a red light, I needed a game plan and asked two ladies in front of me if they had any suggestions. They turned out to be very friendly, and after walking and talking, they asked me if I would like to join their group. We arrived at a restaurant right on the water. Hours passed with great conversation.

By late evening, the majority of the group headed home, and the three of us walked uphill towards the Sky Tower. After a few drinks, we searched for Mexican food, which I thought was an American thing, but is apparently common worldwide.

We overindulged on a few different things. My addiction to chips and salsa again winning the battle vs will power. I headed back to the hotel about midnight hoping not to have a stomach hemorrhage overnight. Being found in boxers with chewed up chips and salsa oozing out of me is not how I would prefer to leave this world.

The day was a whirlwind but ended with new friends in a foreign country. One of them was so kind and welcoming, she met me a couple of other days and drove me around Auckland. I am happy to say that we stay in touch to this day via social media. Saying "hello" to people around the globe is the best contribution social media has made to society.

Meeting people in foreign countries is a part of traveling I really enjoy. Though there are occasionally differences in lingo, customs and social norms, people are very similar everywhere I have been. Some love their careers; others hate their jobs. Some love to write; others see it as punishment. Night clubs, libraries, dog rescues, amusement parks, sports and concerts are universal. So are the interests of people.

I woke up the next morning to countless texts from friends and family in the U.S. Overnight, there had been a massive earthquake in New Zealand, and they were assuming it may have been where I was staying. Apparently, Murphy's Law is my travel companion.

I slept through the night, undisturbed, but realized it didn't mean there wasn't an earthquake. Reaching for the window curtains, I wondered if opening them would reveal a city in ruins and madness while I managed to sleep through it all. Immediately, it was clear that Auckland was unaffected by the quake. Wellington and Christchurch were both hit hard. By the end of my trip, it was clear that possibly the *only* negative of life in New Zealand is the frequency of earthquakes.

I pondered traveling to those cities to help in some way. Local news indicated that roads and airports leading to them were closed. Authorities were asking people to stay out of those areas, and requested people donate various items to help victims instead.

I totally understand why city officials often refuse volunteer help immediately after disasters. In the United States, this is an era where classless criminals participate in looting of businesses during disasters, treating tragic circumstances like shopping sprees.

That's the real disaster in all of this. Horrific storms and earthquakes are unavoidable parts of life, just random bad luck. Hordes of people profiting from the situation like parasites is a uniquely human thing. There is no lower life-form then those who steal non-necessities when society is disrupted by catastrophes.

I needed to get a workout in. It was Saturday, and the park I chose was bustling. Using a picnic table as my base of operations, I dove into my usual travel plan: sets of push-ups and lunges.

To my left, a thirty-something woman played fetch with her dog. To my right, a cricket team was practicing. Scattered everywhere else were people doing "park things." Dropping for a set of push-ups, my hand went into a warm, slimy deposit. I now know the body temperature of canine intestines is similar to that of morning coffee—a reminder that dogs do "park things" as well.

I snatched my hand away, as though it was a cobra. I immediately wiped my hand off in the surrounding grass as though I could undo it by wiping quickly. This process would be repeated after realizing several times that I didn't get it all.

Disturbed dog poo has asbestos-like qualities. It's not dangerous until released into the air, after which it becomes exponentially more powerful—like a bad smell rolling down a hill gaining momentum.

After relocating to another table, and inspecting the grounds for brown, pungent land mines, I hammered the workout and sat to watch the goings-on at the park.

As an American sports fan, I was fascinated by the sport of cricket. It is similar to baseball but with the pitcher having a running start. I chatted briefly with an older man who was sitting on a bench taking in the cricket practice. He was a Brit, about 70 years old with a white beard. Friendly, in a salty way, he was in Auckland visiting his son who was coaching the cricket team.

The 2016 presidential election in the U.S. had taken place four days earlier. He busted my chops about the result. "How could you let that happen?" he said. I appreciated his confidence in my superpower of altering election results.

I immediately replied in a very casual way, "We followed the plan the British used to block Brexit." My reply earned respect. Apparently, he enjoys a volley of verbal crap-slinging. He laughed, slapped me on the back and said, "Cheers!"

We had a fun, rollicking conversation. He opined that the U.S. was in decline and its population over-obsessed with celebrities and social media. I completely agreed but pointed out that gossip rags originated in Britain. He said, "The U.S. originated in Britain too!" We laughed.

He predicted that at some point the U.S. would get financially overextended and have to become a member nation, not the world leader. I replied that was yet another British invention, and he laughed hysterically. Slapping his thighs, rocking forward and backward, he told me, "For an American, you aren't too bad." A compliment—I think.

A love of sports is universal. The only variance is which sports are popular in a given country. In the United States, many sports teams are the favorite entrée of the city's menu. In some cities, baseball is king; in others, it is football. Fans of other sports have their strong-holds as well.

For many sports, the leagues in the U.S. are the best in the world. Playing in the U.S. is the goal for most foreign baseball, basketball and hockey players. There are plenty of options in other countries, but MLB and the NBA have the highest level of competition—the playground of the elite.

The NFL is an outlier due to American football not being a global professional sport. The Super Bowl champions declare themselves "World Champions," a true but misleading statement. Why not Galactic Champions? Universal Champs? There is no team on Venus that can handle the New England Patriots. The Cleveland Browns may lose to some Martians though.

Conversing with this man was interesting. He was an enormous fan of a sport that really does not exist in the U.S. This trip was immediately after the Chicago Cubs had won their first World Series championship in over 100 years. No longer the punchline to baseball jokes, they were the talk of sports in the U.S. I asked the gentleman if he followed baseball at all.

He had no idea there was a team called the Cubs—a good reminder that the sports world does not revolve around United States, nor should it.

Following the work out, I walked the downtown area for hours until I had a good feel for a couple of square miles in Auckland. Back at the hotel for a siesta, I made a decision about plans for the next day. Something I always wanted to do was available just outside of Auckland. I made the reservation for the next morning. This would be epic.

The shuttle picked me up at the Sky Tower at 10am. After picking up other passengers, nine of us were taken about an hour's drive outside of Auckland. 48 years old at the time, I was the oldest of the skydiving group by at least 20 years. I am not sure if skydiving is for the young, or if most people my age have more sense.

Of the group planning to jump out of an airplane that day, I was the only English-speaking member. Through a combination of charades, talking, laughing and failing miserably, I found out the rest of the group was Japanese. So much for a conversation.

We arrived at a small hangar and were taken inside. After watching a safety video, we put on blue jump suits—kind of a onesie for adults.

I stepped into the first one I was handed and pulled it up. I realized it was too small when I heard a tearing sound. The employee, a young lady, laughed and said, "Let's try another size."

It would be a tandem jump, meaning I would be harnessed to a certified skydiving professional who would do all of the work. All I had to do was stay attached and try not to soil the onesie in flight.

My tandem guide had just landed from a previous jump. Professional skydivers are in a volume business. In good weather, they will get as many jumps in a day as possible. He walked in the hangar and handed the open parachute to a staff member who immediately began repacking it. He introduced himself as "Mike," and we walked toward the plane.

An airplane can be described as a metal tube full of people. Most commercial planes are so big the passengers don't necessarily notice that is the case.

This plane was absolutely a metal tube full of people— a very skinny tube outfitted for skydiving. There was one long bench running right down the middle of the plane. Everyone sat on that bench with a jump guide directly behind them. Fortunately, for awkwardness reasons, they don't really cinch their harness to yours until right before the jump. Having gotten into the plane first, my guide and I would be the last out of the plane.

While we were prepping in the hangar, a crew of people arrived with their own gear. That was the interesting thing about this group: they did not have much gear.

Each of them had a personalized helmet adorned with a Go Pro camera.

And shoes.

In between the headwear and footwear there was only one article of clothing, and it was not a jumpsuit. These guys were wearing only briefs.

All levels of humility exist across the human spectrum. These guys were as uninhibited as a sober person can be. Part of me admired the "who cares" attitude. Few people are willing to stray from what is "normal," yet it was odd at the same time. Walking around in public, wearing only briefs, *is* the opposite of what everyone else is doing.

We all live in a world where behavior is easily classified as normal or abnormal. The strange, or abnormal, behavior stands out. A good example is the normal behavior on elevators. Everyone gets on and either looks up or down while facing forward. Small talk is tolerated, but that is as edgy as it gets.

A famous sociology experiment once had a person get into elevators with his back facing the doors. Everyone else, of course, faced the doors looking up or down. The study examined people's reactions to the one person doing the exact opposite of everyone else. People on the elevator were thrown for a loop.

Some of them also turned their back to the doors, not wanting to be different. In a crowded elevator, he just stood out as the oddball. Imagine the person standing behind him, inexplicably face to face with the *only person* facing that direction.

Abnormal behavior is always noticed.

During college, I was in the elevator of a parking garage with three friends. It was a double date, with all four of us knowing each other well. My good friend Dave, tall at 6' 5," was always easy to spot. He was a hilarious guy and things often flowed toward mischief when I was with him. Often when Dave laughed, his eyes would be shut with his mouth hanging open, silent the whole time. The silent laughter would be disrupted by an occasional gasp for air, after which he continued to laugh without a sound until the next gasp.

As the elevator stopped on each floor, it got more and more crowded. Eventually getting to the point where, as soon as the doors opened, whomever was waiting would see the abject lack of space and wave us along. Thankfully.

Common sense is a beautiful thing.

At the next stop, a family of five was waiting. As the doors opened and both groups looked at each other, the mother was totally undeterred by the lack of space.

Leading her brood into the elevator was only possible if everyone in it shifted and adjusted, cussing under their breath at being forced to do so.

This is where having a friend with no "filter" would come in handy. That friend would blurt out something incredibly blunt, rude and true, possibly ending the situation. Unfortunately, no one on the elevator brought that friend along. The mother stepped into the elevator and the ducklings followed. The space being so crowded, their entry into it took some time.

As the middle child—probably five or six years old—followed along, the doors began to close. This being an American elevator, liability concerns dictated the design. The doors were lined with thick black rubber bumpers to ensure that anything closed between them would not be injured. Impact with the bumpers would send the doors back from where they came.

The young boy was unaware of the doors closing. He turned his body sideways to wedge himself into the elevator. Facing inward toward his mother, he was not watching the doors.

I suppose the adults nearest the doors, or his father from behind, all assumed someone else would touch the bumpers and buy the children more time to get in but no one did.

The boy was bumped on both sides by the doors which immediately bounced open with no harm done. It's possible the impact could've broken an egg, but the child was nothing more than scared. We've all seen kids fall down and cry, uninjured but startled, freaked out that one moment they're walking and the next they have grass up their nose.

In this case, the boy froze for half a second after impact with the doors, unsure what just happened. Then he began to cry. This was an instance where laughter was *totally* unacceptable. Though the mother showed questionable judgment—or vision problems—trying to get on the elevator, laughing at a crying child is taboo.

That's what's funny about the human condition. Sometimes the urge to use the restroom strikes at the most inconvenient times. Hunger slaps you in the face when no food is available. And, sometimes, you just have to laugh.

While in college, I once saw a fellow student fall down some icy steps. He legitimately could've been hurt, yet the sight of him shrieking and launching a handful of books into the air as he went down was pure comedy.

I skated over to him to see if he was okay. Genuinely concerned, I couldn't even speak without laughing, making my concern appear very dubious. I apologized for laughing while still laughing.

Fortunately, the fallen dude shared my humor. I helped him pick up his books, we laughed about it, and off he went. It would've been perfect karma for him to see the next 10 seconds of my life. Traversing across the ice that took him down, I was a cyclone of flailing arms and legs trying to avoid the same fate—the entertainment for a couple of young ladies passing by who giggled at my struggles.

As the elevator doors recoiled away from the boy, containing the laughter was priority one. It would've been a perfect time to be shorter. Plastered against the back wall, I perhaps could have snickered in silence had I been hidden by the bodies of those in front of me. At 6'3", my head hovered above many in the elevator. Both of our dates were to my right, and Dave was trapped against the side wall of the elevator on that side.

The young boy started wailing, and his mother turned to him. I was overcome by the desire to laugh. Knowing I couldn't, I looked down and tried to hold it in. We have all been there. Vomiting and laughing aren't close cousins, but they share one trait; when you really have to do either, holding it in is nearly impossible.

I was looking down, biting my lower lip. My shoulders bouncing betrayed my attempts to stifle it. I was trying to talk myself off of the ledge of laughing, but it was like a sneeze coming on. More and more, you realize it's going to happen.

The mother was showing grave concern for her son. The boy was screaming as though he had lost a limb. The dad was now holding the doors open, while the mother was squatting beside the child talking to him.

The one thing I absolutely should *not* have done was look at Dave. We had a way of communicating just by throwing glances, and an eruption of laughter was likely. To avoid losing my composure would be a miracle. Knowing I shouldn't, I was dying to see what Dave thought of all of this. The people crammed among us were respectfully quiet. This situation was far from dire, proven when the boy stopped crying on demand when given candy.

The candy, sadly, did not arrive quickly enough. Caving to temptation, I looked up and to my right. Taller than me, Dave's head was visible for all to see. I don't even think Dave saw me glance his way—laughing with one's eyes closed makes that difficult. He was in the midst of a full-blown episode of silent laughter. Immediately upon seeing it, I exploded.

Unfortunately for me, I don't laugh silently. This was well beyond giggling. Hearing me laugh only accelerated Dave's silent celebration. His body convulsed in a space with no room for that, followed immediately by the inevitable gasp for air.

The mother turned toward me scornfully. "How can you laugh at this?" she asked bitterly. Strangely, the dad looked at me with no objection. Perhaps he had become numb to overreaction. Maybe he is a member of my unfortunate club—those who laugh when they shouldn't. At this point, others in the elevator tempted to laugh may have stifled theirs when they saw Mom's reaction. Or they thought we were jerks for laughing.

By this time the "candy for silence" swap had taken place and the boy was completely composed. The family stepped out of the elevator and said they would wait for the next one. My date had planted her left elbow in my ribs like machine gun fire for my clear violation of elevator etiquette.

The dudes wearing only underwear got on the plane last. My jump guide said the "briefers" routinely pay for the flight but jump without a tandem guide. They have been doing it for years, jumping countless times.

Always in their briefs.

The hypersensitive atmosphere in the United States would likely judge these people as criminals. In New Zealand, they were regular customers—an interesting look at what societies tolerate from place to place.

It took the small plane a while to get to 15,000 feet of altitude. Combined, the scantily clad and those of us wearing onesies totaled about 20.

When the time arrived, tandem harnesses were tightened. The jump bay door opened and the crew in briefs scooted forward. I was strangely calm, not concerned at all that anything would go wrong, just excited for the freefall. As the "briefers" jumped from the plane, they took their time to create space between skydivers before the next one jumped.

The last one of the group decided to jump out backwards. He stood up in the jump bay door and turned to face the rest of us. Perched half in and half out of the plane, we were shown the power of a strong updraft.

The guy was not badly out of shape, but he had a layer of insulation that likely equaled an extra 10 pounds. The updraft grabbed that 10 pounds and his gut shimmied up-and-down like stadium spectators doing "the wave" as fast as possible. I am not sure if that was his plan. It may have been an unintended consequence of standing the way he did. It was quite a display.

At that altitude, with the door open, the ambient noise was loud. Over that, I could hear laughter from those even closer to the gyrating stomach fat. Anyone nervous about the jump was likely calmed down by the "belly dance" from a guy wearing only Fruit of the Looms.

One at a time, our group left the plane. Eventually we had scooted as far as the bench could take us. My guide Mike yelled, "You ready?" A split second after my "thumbs up," we were doing a forward roll out of the plane at 15,000 feet.

To control the fall, skydivers assume a face-down "starfish" position. I will never forget that experience; it is still incredibly vivid. Our freefall lasted nearly a minute. By Mike's choosing, we started a fast counter clockwise spin.

I could see how many jumpers could lose their breakfast. Staring straight down brought a dizzying effect. Mike stopped the spin, and we had about thirty seconds of plummeting toward Earth. Aware we were falling fast, there was no panic. As land rushed up to meet us, I did quickly debate what happens to one if the 'chute doesn't open.

People have had that fate and survived. I am not sure how. As a kid, I saw a TV show that featured a clip of a skydiving competition which was underway. The skydivers were trying to land inside a target on the ground. One jumper was blown astray by the wind. He sailed beyond the target and over a fence into some water, then there were screams. He had landed in a gator habitat.

Landing off target in Australia could be a major issue. In New Zealand, only landing on a busy road would lead to trouble.

When Mike pulled our 'chute, the immediate deceleration felt like we climbed upwards. The jump zone was an idyllic place. As we slowly descended, to my right was the Tasman Sea, and on my left, the South Pacific. This was a mad rush of adrenaline, lasting an amazing five minutes.

As we neared the ground, it seemed we were moving faster than planned. The driver that picked us up explained to a passenger that the landings were easy. Mike told me the oldest person he had tandem jumped with was in her early 80s, just a few months earlier.

Mike had it all under control. The deep grass of the field made the landing soft as a pillow. The frailest elderly person would've walked away. As we stood up and walked to the hangar, the guys in briefs rowdied about with one another and were heading to an airplane to go back up. We got inside the hangar to take off the onesies, and that quickly, Mike was meeting his next jumper and off he went.

He told me the most jumps he had in a day was just over 20. He clearly loves to fly. I am jealous that he gets to do it so often, though it likely loses some allure when you're doing it to pay the bills. I certainly plan to do it again.

Fully-clothed of course.

I have always loved parks. As a kid the playground equipment trumped all and as I got a little older, I played Little League baseball and "backyard" football in parks all the time.

Now, parks reflect the quality of the community around them. It's not an entirely fair statement as parks require financial support that favors some communities over others. Parks in affluent areas gleam brighter than those elsewhere. Either way, parks are peaceful places—no place better to sip coffee and watch ducks waddle about. This shift inside me is a constant reminder of the aging process.

I appreciated parks in my 20s but spent very little time there. The hustle of building a career and maintaining a social life left little time for sitting and taking things in. Now, I love to just sit in a park after a workout and refocus on my day and my priorities.

In New Zealand, parks are called "domains." The ones in Auckland are a wonderland for park lovers. The Auckland Domain sits adjoining a university. I wandered the domain for hours, revisiting places I had already been, watching people play fetch with dogs, or catch with one another. There were people enjoying picnics scattered about. I headed back to the hotel thinking that was as nice a park as I had ever seen. As with most things, I would soon be proven wrong.

As a fan of American football, Sundays in the fall and early winter are revered. Due to time zone differences, the games beginning at noon U.S. central time start during the morning rush on Monday in New Zealand.

After watching the round of early games, I headed for an epic walkabout. There were two more domains on my list for that day. It would take a full day of walking and would certainly justify the pizza I planned for that night.

The first domain on my route was the Mt. Eden Domain.

It took me nearly two hours to get there. The Mt. Eden Domain is the site of a crater—once an active volcano that Mother Nature has reclaimed and filled with grass. This crater was once the mouth of New Zealand's tallest volcano which, due to its size, was once used as a defensive position by the native New Zealanders, the Maori tribe.

During my visit, the edge of the crater was ringed with people. It was more of a historical site than a traditional park. No "park things" were seen there aside from a large dog squatting and pooping, which, as you might imagine, I seemed to notice more often.

Eden Garden is a place plant lovers would adore. Sitting on over five acres, it showcases the variety of remarkable plant life New Zealand offers. The Mt. Eden Domain and Eden Garden, sit within Mount Eden Village, an incredibly charming community of small shops and stores that look like they belong in a snow globe—my favorite kind of place.

A longer walk led me to an even more amazing spot—the One Tree Hill Domain. It was not easy to find. Google maps and my iPhone were fooled, leaving me to improvise. Shop owners likely snickered as I walked back and forth like a windshield wiper in search of the street that ultimately did not exist.

Stopping outside of a convenience store, I asked a man pumping gas how to get there. He alternated laughing with taking a drag on a cigarette and pointed me in the right direction. I was a bit unnerved by both his laughing and the poor judgement of smoking while pumping gas. Perhaps that was why he was laughing.

Finally arriving at the One Tree Hill Domain, I was only sure I was in right place because of the sign affirming it.

What I saw did not look like any park I had visited before. Like the Mount Eden Domain, the One Tree Hill Domain sits atop a dormant volcano. Seemingly endless pasture land stretched from the domain's entrance to the obelisk at the very top. Sheep and cows walked about everywhere with furry babies scurrying to keep up with their mamas.

I hesitated, thinking I had walked into a neighboring property. I looked back at the entrance and could see the sign advertising the domain. Looking forward again, it looked like I was in the middle of a farm. I froze for a couple of minutes trying to take all of this in.

Again remembering the advice of veteran travelers, "do what the locals do," I looked around to see dozens of people walking amongst the sheep and cattle. I *was* in the right place—it was just a different kind of place. A park with livestock and people all intermingled.

As I walked into the domain, completely baffled and impressed by where I was, sheep bleated to one another and distant "mooooos" were heard. The animals, so conditioned to human interaction, were completely nonplussed by my presence. It was incredible.

This was as close as I'll *ever* come to being a farmer. With all love and respect to farmers, there would be a famine of a biblical scale if I was in charge of growing food. Even with limited farming skills, I know that where there are cows, there are typically bulls. Bars around the world offer "Ladies Night" drink specials knowing men will arrive to pay full price because the ladies are there. Mixing among genders is not confined to any species.

I felt a bolt of adrenaline when the possibility of bulls being nearby occurred to me.

As a high school senior, I visited property belonging to my aunt and uncle. The area was farther out in the county, and much less densely populated. Much of the area was still farm land. My aunt, uncle and two cousins had moved out there about a decade earlier. The land and house had been in my aunt's family, and the property totaled about 30 acres.

My parents purchased three of those acres. On their property was a tranquil spot with a weeping willow tree near a pond. I awoke that Saturday morning sore from a football game the night before but in a great mood. We won the game, and I had gotten a "yes" from a stunning girl when I asked if she would be my homecoming date.

To a teenage boy, winning football games and smooth sailing on the dating front were all that was necessary to wake up in a great mood, and I wanted to savor the good fortune under the willow tree.

I drove out there and parked near the barn. I had called prior to coming, but no one answered—a common result in the pre-cell phone and texting era. Knowing they wouldn't care, I parked on their property. The fields were peaceful and quiet as I went through a gate and walked a few acres away from the road to the willow tree and pond.

I spent a nice hour or so out there. The weather was perfect for sitting and enjoying a quiet spot. Making this kind of an effort to enjoy nature was unusual for me. At 18, I was far from a deep thinker. My thought process was an endless cycle of thought about girls, sports and food. Taking in nature like a poet simply never happened. What exactly took me out there that day is honestly beyond me even now,

After sitting there for a while, I got restless. Hunger had once again guided my thoughts; as I headed back to my car I noticed a significant change. A neighboring farmer used some of the families' land for his cattle to graze. When I arrived, there were no cows or bulls in sight; in fact, I had forgotten they may be there.

Unfortunately, they now filled the fields I had to walk through, and this made me justifiably uneasy. I had absolutely no farming or ranching instincts, but I knew the anatomical and temperamental differences between a cow and bull.

I wanted to get to my car as fast as possible while also drawing no attention to myself. I could have taken a longer route, far away from the herd, but I was a teenager directed by the belief that nothing bad will happen to *me*—bull stompings happen to *other* people.

I took the most direct path to the car, right through about 1/3 of the herd. I walked faster which wasn't easy in longer pasture grass, and kept my head on a swivel looking for trouble. I carried my Sony Walkman with "old school" headphones running a half circle over my head.

I looked to my right and saw one animal a good distance away had seemingly taken an interest in me, or appeared to. The majority of the herd chewed and "mooed" without seeming to care, not even moving. This one was walking right toward me. I picked up my pace to a slight trot, telling myself there was nothing to worry about while simultaneously worrying.

I looked back to my right to check the progress. From a distance, I wasn't sure if it was a cow or bull but assumed the worst. It too had begun to trot and was coming right at me. I took this to be a bad sign, so I started to run.

So did the bull.

Fortunately, the fence was only a ten second sprint ahead, unfortunately the bull was only a ten second sprint behind. There would be no way to get to the actual gate, nor to climb the fence if the bull kept coming. The fence drew closer. It was a stockade fence with horizontal planks, each separated by a gap—your typical pasture enclosure.

Being sore while running through tall grass doesn't help one's speed, but fear certainly does. I got a few steps away from the fence and looked back. I *really* hoped the bull had stopped, satisfied he had scared the cowardly intruder into a sprint, maybe even mockingly snorting at me.

He hadn't.

There was no hope of me jumping and clearing the fence, but all I had to do was get most of me over it and let gravity do the rest. Whatever part of my legs hit the fence would cause me to flip and land in some bizarre, maybe gruesome, way. Not getting to the fence would *definitely* be gruesome; so I jumped as high as I could. I clipped the fence with my right knee, tumbled over it and landed hard with a strange grunt. Still lying there totally adrenalized, I looked over to the fence a few feet away. The bull stood there looking through the planks, snorting victoriously.

I got up and assessed the damage. There was nothing major; the resiliency of youth is a beautiful thing. I dusted myself off, talked a little trash to the bull and realized my headphones were no longer with me. The Walkman made the flight, but I never saw the headphones again. I bought new ones on the way home, and as teenagers are famous for, told my parents nothing of it.

That memory lingered as I walked among this herd. Could this unique park possibly have bulls? No country in the world is as liability conscious as the United States. Even laid-back countries like New Zealand, where common sense is seen as an expectation, would likely not let bulls and people within the same fence line.

Assuredly, we were about to find out. If ever there was to be a video capturing a crazed man hurdling sheep, trying to evade a bull, this would be it. Fortunately for me, and the sheep I would have to hurdle, there didn't appear to be any bulls. I was definitely not going to do "visual checks" around the pasture.

I chose to hang in the area with no cows.

There were many more sheep than cows, and they ranged all over the One Tree Hill Domain. The area was really fascinating. A low laying area to one side was a field where people spelled out names and initials using field stones. On the other side, was a pasture with vividly green terraces leading upward like a grassy staircase to the upper area I was in.

It was a truly spectacular setting. The local residents are extraordinarily lucky to be able to hop in a car and be there in minutes, every day if they like. Due to the domain being atop a volcano, there were spectacular views looking down at Auckland and the sea. The Sky Tower stood proudly, easy to spot. From that view, I could tell by its size it was going to be a l-o-n-g walk back.

As I started to make my way toward the exit, I came upon a woman walking her dog. The dog had an interesting brindle coat and was hyper-focused on sniffing clover while his dog mom waited impatiently. We chatted; she was extraordinarily friendly and helpful, answering my many questions. I was intrigued about the domain and who took care of the animals.

She said the sheep and cattle were property of the city and are cared for by a division of the park service. They were well-cared for in every way by the local government.

I explained to her how unique and unusual that was from my experience in the U.S. and raved to her about how much I loved Auckland. As she loaded her dog into the back of the SUV, I thanked her for the chat and wished her a good day. It was now late afternoon, and I had a multiple hour walk ahead of me—longer if I got lost, which was likely.

A quick conversation unfolded when she asked me if I had walked there. When she found out I had, she quickly and insistently offered to drive me home. My journey was beyond the 10-mile mark already. I typically hate accepting favors from people. I love being on the other end of it, doing nice things, but will go to extreme lengths to avoid being a burden. My immediate refusal of the ride was squashed by her enthusiasm and willingness to help.

When she found out I was staying beside the Sky Tower, she thought I was completely bereft of common sense for wanting to continue on foot. She happily drove me well past Mount Eden Village, where her family lived, all the way to my hotel. Happy as can be, she was not the least bit concerned about loading a complete stranger into her car.

There are certainly people that generous and kind in every country. Many folks would be glad to provide that same favor if they could be assured the friendly stranger could be trusted. Short of knowing that, scenarios like this are increasingly rare in the U.S.

Though there are plenty of amazing people living in the U.S., the amount of crime and inexplicably awful acts of violence there make people far less trusting. Understandable, but sadly true.

On the ride home, she called her daughter to make dinner arrangements. Hearing only one side of the story, it sounded like a typical mother/teen daughter conversation. The original type of pizza and restaurant mentioned by the mom were unacceptable to the teen. They were "gross and disgusting" in that order, according to her mom's replay. The daughter's friend had recommended a place, so Mom acquiesced.

Another great part of traveling is simply watching the daily interactions and routines in which people all over the world participate. It is worth noting again, the vast majority of the developed world is *w-a-y* more similar than different.

When friends and I discuss travel, which happens constantly, it often favors destinations known for great food. My podcast, the Peanut Butter and Passports Podcast, is typically about either traveling or food. Maybe both.

These conversations tend to focus on the legendary culinary centers such as Paris or nearly anywhere in Italy. A recent interview with two chefs pointed out that Lyon, France, is a hotbed of culinary innovation and the birthplace of many top chefs in the world today.

I have a friend who describes meals he has eaten in Florence, Italy, so well, I feel like I have eaten them too. It is incredibly good for me that I love to work out because I really love to eat. If that day comes when the body betrays me and legitimate, intense workouts are no longer possible, I may just have to become a sumo wrestler.

I think Europe is the focus of many Americans' travel plans in part due to the culinary scene many countries there are famous for. If you specifically filter out food as a factor and ask people what the most beautiful place they've ever seen is, answers are scattered across the globe.

Of course, Victoria Falls is the choice for some. There are vistas and photos captured in Safari areas that cannot be replicated anywhere else. A great sunset over the ocean is preposterously cool and explains why so many people like to sit on the beach and drink. The quality of the sunset, naturally, rises in direct proportion with their blood/alcohol content. Sunsets are a great thing to love because they are available every day.

Since my first visits to the Andes, and then the Rockies, mountains have always been the view I enjoy the most. I know someone that owns a condominium on the beach in Florida. If they chose, they could sit on the balcony and relax or work with a smashing view every day. And they should.

Many people prefer urban settings. Central Park in New York City breaks up the concrete jungle, providing a refuge for those needing some green. Pictures taken by underwater photographers reveal an almost alien environment in our oceans. Having been blessed to stand on the floor of the Pacific Ocean, I can attest to the crazily cartoonish look some fish have. Naturally, the fish likely consider me cartoonish looking as well.

Pictures of the Rainbow Mountains in China are so colorful they look altered. The Northern Lights, Norwegian fjords and Antarctica also provide vistas that make a person sit still in disbelief. There are rock formations in Utah that demonstrate the crazy beauty that nature provides. As do the Grand Canyon, Redwood National Park and too many other amazing places to list.

Ultimately there is no correct answer, just personal preference, but it's a fun debate to have.

New Zealand consists of two islands: the north and south. Auckland sits on the north island, and a trip spent entirely on the north island would make for a stunning visit.

Most personal accounts and reviews of trips to New Zealand tend to rave about the very same spot. A single place in New Zealand that has blown people's minds across the globe sits on the south island: the city of Queenstown.

I can think back about the places I have traveled and recreate in my "minds-eye" certain shots or views that are beyond description. Queenstown dominates those memories.

It sits in the southern third of that island—not a coastal city but one built lakeside, perched on the shore of Lake Wakatipu. Much more like a quaint mountain town than a city, it only has a population of 15,000 people.

If at some point you need a vacation that will truly reset your patience, goals, view of the world or anything else nagging at you, visit Queenstown. On the flight there, I was noticeably excited, and that is rare. I look forward to things a great deal, but actual excitement generally eludes me.

I had read and studied so much about the city after booking the trip, I feared it would fail to measure up to unfair expectations—a concern that proved to be silly.

Waiting at the airport for my flight, I spotted a man wearing a Seattle Seahawks baseball cap. We struck up a conversation about that team, American football and many other things that spurred him to book the trip. His was not an unusual tale by any stretch; it was merely a reminder of how far-flung travelers are and how small the world has become in the 21st century.

While we chatted in New Zealand, thousands of planes were in the air, crisscrossing Earth, taking people of all origins to places of all types. The number of people I would end up meeting in Queenstown from all over the planet left an impression. A reminder to live, not merely exist. A fixation to see things before either it, or I, are gone. To spread the "*Wow*" factor of those sites in the hopes of motivating people to travel, or, at the very least, skydive in their briefs.

I love to read while traveling. I typically take multiple books with the hope of coming back with none of them. It sounds a bit nutty to give away books, but it comes from a good place. The hideous Sandy Hook Elementary school shooting happened in Connecticut in 2012. Multiple staff members and very young students were killed by yet another crazed, heavily armed, assault-rifle-toting American.

In the aftermath, a media personality suggested we all practice random acts of kindness in honor of those victims. Social media helped this movement become viral. It made me wonder why I needed that outside impetus to do very simple things that make others smile. I am now a faithful devotee to that movement and the positivity it passes forward.

One idea that came to mind was what to do with books when I'm finished reading them.

Before the trip, I prepared Post-it notes and put them inside the books. My handwriting looks like that of a caffeinated chimpanzee, so it took an extraordinary effort to make it legible. The message was simple; it had to be. Post-it notes are like a paper version of Twitter—there is very little space for rambling.

Each note indicated that I loved the book myself and left it intentionally for someone else to enjoy. I told them if they found this, it was theirs to keep if they wanted it. I did suggest they do the same when they're finished with it.

Personally, I would love to find a book in that fashion. One that, on the inside back cover, showed a list of the cities that book was read in. Imagine finding a best seller, or book you love, and upon finishing it, you see that it has been to Tokyo, London, Singapore, Sydney and Cape Town with different readers.

Granted that might send a germaphobe reeling, requiring a 12-hour bath and medical tests after being exposed to foreign cooties; but for most of us, I think that would be a cool experience.

At the airport that day, I had just finished a bestseller, one both inspiring, and sad, titled <u>When Breath Becomes Air</u>. It had the aforementioned notes inside of it. I was carrying it as I walked to a bookstore in the airport to buy another. I came upon two ladies, friends it appeared, that were browsing for books as well. We wound up in the same aisle doing the awkward "Excuse me, pardon me" shuffle that occurs when trying to see books blocked from view by other people.

Realizing they were about to spend money to buy a book, I said, 'Excuse me," and explained my new strategy for sharing books while traveling. I offered it to them, and they were caught pleasantly off guard.

They were happy to take the book, though I'm not sure they read it. No book matches the whim of every reader, but I am hoping they may now do the same with books they've finished.

The only downside to reading is the missed "people watching" opportunities that airports provide. I'm not sure how comedians plan their act or where they come up with material. Just sitting in an airport and looking around is what I'd suggest to any aspiring comedian.

As with any gathering place for large crowds—stadiums, malls etc.—airports have many flavors of people. If "variety is the spice of life," airports are spicy places. Buying coffee before that flight, I was behind a man who looked to be in his 50s or 60s. He did not look old and had an average build and a trimmed white beard. Noticing his polo shirt, jeans and cowboy boots, I wondered what language he would speak when ordering.

It was English, with an accent different than American—likely an Aussie or Kiwi. As he stepped aside waiting for his coffee, I stepped forward and ordered mine. As we both waited, I looked over at him and noticed something that reached out and grabbed my attention.

Part of the "people watching" experience is noticing how other people are comfortable being seen. People today sometimes wear pajama pants while traveling. I sat by a friendly lady once who was returning from a business trip sporting teenage mutant ninja pajamas. She explained her rationale as, "It was a long tough week, and I wanted to be comfortable." I had no issue with it, particularly after her confident assertion that this made perfect sense. But I noticed it because it seemed to break from the norm.

I have since noticed people wearing pajama pants at airports more and more often. Maybe they had always been "hidden in plain sight," and I just started noticing them—similar to noticing dogs pooping in parks after smooshing dog poop with my hand.

Many people were dressed in business attire, likely traveling for business. Most travelers could be described as "dressed casually." That description covers *a lot* of ground. I prefer to dress as I would if I were going out to a nice, but not "white-tablecloth," restaurant. It isn't always possible for many reasons, but that's my goal.

The gentleman standing beside me as we waited for coffee wasn't wearing anything remarkable to either extreme. What was noteworthy was the amount of white chest hair billowing out between the buttons and over-the-top of the collar of his shirt.

It looked like a white Muppet was trying to escape the confines of his shirt.

Clearly, he was comfortable with this. Having chest hair the length of his shoe did not suddenly happen to him the night before.

It reminded me of a time when I was teaching high school history. Between classes, several teachers were standing at an intersection of hallways, supervising. While we were talking, a student walked up to another male teacher to ask him a question.

While chatting, she said, "Oh, you've got a hair," and reached to pull it from his shirt. While trying to remove the stray hair, she realized it wasn't stray. It was still attached to his chest, and it merely poked through between buttons.

I happened to be looking at her face when the gruesomely awkward reality struck her. She was quite dramatic in her disgust, squealing and moving about strangely as far away from us as she could—as though distance would "undo" the entire incident.

The group of teachers completely lost all composure as the poor girl ducked into a bathroom, presumably to wash her hands and maybe plan a 12-hour bath after school that day.

Fortunately for me, the man, after receiving his coffee, simply walked away. Had he hovered over the table where milk, sugar and other coffee enhancers were located, I'm not sure I could have used any of those things. It wouldn't be worth the risk that a white chest hair the length of a spaghetti noodle might fall into my coffee.

As we flew over a stretch of ocean between the Kiwi islands, I knew this was the final week of this trip, and I vowed to make it memorable.

The short flight landed, and a cabby whisked me to my lodging. It was a basement apartment of a house a mile from the heart of Queenstown. The homeowners, a couple likely in their 60s, were incredibly nice. She offered to make me breakfast each morning, and they both offered rides to town frequently.

I chose to walk the mile, sometimes more than once each day. The weather for that week was cool, in the 50s and 60s F (about 15 C), so having layers and rain gear with me at all times would be smart.

But it didn't happen.

My first visit to the downtown area had three objectives:

1 – get acquainted with the street layout

2 – visit the lakeshore

3 – grab coffee

Coffee shop hounding is a favorite pastime of mine, and Queenstown had a great spot called the Vudu Café. While most tourists packed into Starbucks, the locals love Vudu. I had to work out *and* walk five miles daily to deal with the assortment of culinary dreams the Vudu Café offered. When coffee or a snack was needed, Vudu was my place.

However, Starbucks was a great place to meet other tourists. Solo travel sounds awful to some people, and for them it may be a bad choice. Personally, I enjoy it. If meeting people and swapping stories is the goal, Starbucks is a good place. I prefer local shops, but many traveling solo do so armed with laptops. Starbucks welcomes them—the number of power outlets confirms it.

I met several people at Starbucks when in the mood for conversation during that week. We met up on other days for coffee, hikes and the like. Other solo travelers are often like-minded and typically up for hijinks or conversation.

Though the Vudu Café was great, there was a different spot that I was drawn back to multiple times: The

Beach Bar Café, which sits right on the shore. Though the name sounds generic and would seem to be decorated in thatch, parrots and surfboards, it was actually a true café with French leanings. I always found food there to enjoy, along with a postcard view.

One of the waitresses, a citizen of the world, was French and moved to New Zealand for the adventure and English immersion.

Four people sat beside me once: two couples at, or near, retirement age. They were Aussies, and they insisted I join them. This was another great conversation. They were interested in my solo traveling escapades while also speaking of their visits to the U.S. Much of the time it felt like friends talking more than strangers meeting one another.

They asked if I had eaten at Fergburgers, an iconic restaurant in Queenstown. I had read plenty about Fergburgers ahead of time and planned to eat there until I saw the line. Each time I went by, the line extended well outside of the door and past a couple of neighboring stores. You'd have the thought The Beatles were resurrected and playing inside. To accommodate, they have crazy hours for a burger joint: 8am–5am. I am sure the army of drunkards they serve burgers to at 3am are good comedy.

I cruised by the place every day at various times, and there was always a line. Queenstown is too fabulous a city to worry about eating at a certain place. Waiting in a long line just because a place has good food was also unappealing. I don't feel cheated by not having the Fergburger experience.

Queenstown advertises itself as "The Southern Hemisphere's premier four-season lake and alpine resort." Lake Wakatipu is a surreal place. Several shades of blue paint the water, with mountains providing the immediate backdrop. There is a reason Hollywood has used this area in the making of movies set in a far away, fantastic land.

From the Beach Bar Café, there is a walking path that juts out into the lake. Follow this path and Queenstown's Main Street area is blocked from view by the trees. From this part of town, there are houses dotting the hillside with views of the water and mountains that are simply fabulous.

People living in one of those houses would find working from home a struggle because of its ridiculous brilliance.

Queenstown also is hailed as the "Adventure Capital of the World." If the incredible setting isn't enough to attract travelers, the local government has made it nearly impossible to resist visiting with their menu of unique experiences.

Visitors can choose from options including jet boating, bungee jumping, white water rafting, skydiving and paragliding. If that is not enough, there is a massive swing available as well. Aside from that, all there is to do is golfing, skiing, visiting spas, touring wineries, hiking, biking, taking scenic flights or guided tours and stargazing.

A fairly dull place.

Having already experienced skydiving near Auckland, I ponied up to go paragliding. The difference between the two is where you jump from. Skydivers tumble out of airplanes, typically from far higher altitudes. Paragliders find fixed high points, typically cliffs, near safe landing zones to jump off of.

The crew I was paragliding with met at an outfitters store in the downtown area of Queenstown. We were hustled away in a shuttle, picking up others along the way. The destination was about 30 minutes outside of town atop some cliffs.

The drive was a good time. These would be tandem jumps as well, and the professional paragliders were in the shuttle with us. Meeting all of the paragliding instructors revealed a lot about Queenstown itself. One was from Germany, another from Romania, one from Colorado, an Aussie and two people from South Africa.

A few of them met Kiwi ladies who were studying abroad and returned to New Zealand with them. Some came alone because it was simply where they wanted to live—a move I strongly endorse.

I asked the man from Colorado how difficult the paperwork process was in moving to New Zealand. He said there were steps that had to be followed, but it wasn't a difficult ordeal. He noted that passing an English-speaking test was a requirement. Upon hearing that, a New Zealander aboard spoke up saying, "It must be an easy test, or all of the Kiwis would have to leave!"

When we reached the top of the cliffs, we were geared up and the process was explained. I wore a vest with a harness, part of which extended down to the back of my knees.

The amount of time between gearing up and actually going airborne was shockingly short.

My German instructor said, "Alright now, all I need you to do is run off of the edge of the cliff. When you do, the part of your harness behind your legs becomes a chair you can sit in while we fly. Just run fast, straight off of the cliff, and when we are airborne, pull your knees up into the chair position."

Me: Just . . . run off of the cliff?

Instructor: Yes.

Me: Seriously?

Instructor: Yes.

Me: (long pause) Okay.

Instructor: Just be sure you don't slow down as we get to the edge. That could be a problem.

Me: Got it. What kind of problem?

Guide: Depending upon the wind, if you slow down and we fall off, instead of run off, we could slam into the cliff face.

Me: (longer pause) Okay then, (pause) let's run fast.

Guide: Yes (laughing).

We moved back and to our left, away from the rest of the group. He said to me, "This is plenty of space.

Whenever you are ready, start sprinting." I gave him a "thumbs up" and stared at the approximately 30 meters to the edge of the cliff. This was really strange.

As a kid, many others and I were told similar things by our mothers. When we wanted to do something foolish, because our friends were doing it, Mom logic took over and a typical reply would be, "If your friends jumped off of a cliff, would you?"

Depending upon the dynamic between child and mother, the reply to that question could vary. Only the daftest child would jump off a cliff because his friends did, but kids go through stages of verbal warfare and say all kinds of nonsense just to put up a fight.

I was notorious in our family for trying to get the last word in such debates. Being raised in the spanking era, that proved to be unwise on more than one occasion. Yet, here I was, about to run off of a cliff.

I said, "Let's go!" and took off straight for the edge. The least athletic tuba player in history could skydive. It only requires one to fall out of an airplane. How would the last kid picked in gym class possibly pull off paragliding? I have seen many people try to run in public that should never do so. Being a novice paraglider, I assume they would be told, "This isn't for you."

Perhaps on another cliff, with different wind patterns, the epically slow runners would have no problems. I have no idea.

It was awkward running with someone strapped to you and the goofy chair apparatus slapping me in the back of my legs, but apparently it was fast enough. The last couple of steps before the edge actually never hit the ground. The wind grabbed the parachute and lifted us up, with me running in air.

The guide handled this flight like it was a video game. Each of his hands held a handle, which served as a joystick of sorts. We were able to swoop down to our right, rise up again and swoop down to our left. As incredible as skydiving was, this felt more like what a bird would do.

He said to me during the flight that if we stayed closer to the cliff we could literally stay up there as long as we wanted. The updraft was strong enough to fight gravity and allow for unlimited flying antics.

The danger of staying by the cliff is a sudden change in wind direction. A severe unexpected gust, in a different direction, could splatter us into the cliff. We would then become the multicolored splotch for future paragliders and guides to point out during their flight. "You see that red and blue spot on the cliff over there?

That was a guide and customer from a few years ago. They got a little too close to the cliff."

We were in the air for 15 minutes, only coming down because other clients were waiting for their turn. If choosing between skydiving and paragliding, I would have to choose sky diving as the more memorable experience. The adrenaline rush of jumping out of an airplane and free falling to Earth tops everything.

In fairness, the paragliding flight time lasted three times as long as the skydiving adventure and was well worth the cost. As a kid, I would often jealously watch birds fly. Traveling on airplanes is no simulation of what a bird does. After this trip, I would no longer have to wonder what it was like to fly.

I could remember doing it.

I wanted to go "zorbing," though I am not sure why. It involves being enclosed inside an enormous ball and sent rolling down a hill. A combination that sounds like punishment from medieval times. There were a couple of problems. Getting to the location would be challenging, and the actual zorbing may be better for younger people.

I have loved roller coasters my entire life. In my thirties, my friend Chris, and I, road-tripped to two amusement parks hundreds of miles away for a four-day "coaster-fest." While standing in line for a coaster called "The Beast," some young boys behind us were fascinated that "old guys" like us would like roller coasters.

I explained to them that we were just like them, but older. I told them they would always like roller coasters and explained how awesome it is to take road trips as adults to ride any roller coaster we chose to ride.

These two kids, about 10 years old, were totally geeked up. For them, life never seemed better than learning they could "coaster" through life. They asked how many parks we had been to and a full-blown conversation was on.

I told them of a time I visited Disneyland in my mid-20s with some friends to visit Chris, who was a Marine stationed near San Diego. Completely coincidentally, we arrived on the parks 40th birthday. My friends and I entered Disneyland to find out that birthday cake was being served inside the entrance. We had a piece and made a pact to have more cake each time we saw the cake stands. Figuring we wouldn't be by the main entrance again, we safely assumed we may end up having another piece or two of cake.

We had no idea there were cake stands scattered all throughout the park. This got ugly.

We kept our vow and ate double-digit pieces of cake that day. Many hours later, it was pretty sketchy whether we were going to keep the cake down. Fortunately, we avoided any cake-tastrohies, but it was touch and go.

The boys were now completely enchanted with the life ahead of them. Roller coasters for life! Free cake! We didn't even mention things all young boys dream of, like "no bedtime," "eat what you want," and "making your bed is optional." These young gentlemen had a lot to look forward to.

My most recent trip to an amusement park was at age 40, and my enthusiasm was as strong as ever. I cannot say the same about my equilibrium. Even at that age, I made poor amusement park decisions. There was a ride called "The Highland Fling." It was basically designed like a Ferris wheel lying parallel to the ground.

The "fling" spun as fast as imaginable. If the seat I was in were to break loose from the ride, I may have been flung out of the country. It had always been my favorite non-roller coaster ride.

I went to the amusement park that day with my niece and nephew. It was a weekday, during the summer and not overly crowded or miserably hot. We checked in to see how long the line was at The Highland Fling and were pleasantly surprised to see there wasn't one. We rode it once, got off and noticed there was still no line, so we got right back on.

This was a really, really bad idea.

Perhaps rides like that are harder on the body as we move farther from childhood. Or, perhaps riding twice back-to-back was monumental stupidity. The end result was predictable. Stepping off of the ride for the second time in about five minutes, I really did not feel good. Both dizzy and feeling like I may revisit my breakfast, sitting down sounded phenomenal.

But that would show weakness, and men struggle with that.

So, we walked onward. Fortunately, the kids were immediately well ahead of me, unaware that "Uncle Tom" was weaving and staggering. Eventually the kids found a play area, and I found a bench. Just like the near-miss-bathroom-catastrophe in Hawaii, and the cake-eating-bonanza in California, I managed to dodge an embarrassing fate.

The memory of having my brain scrambled on The Highland Fling rushed to mind as I debated zorbing. While in Starbucks later that day, I spoke with a young American. He was on a trip around the world and had just arrived in New Zealand from Malaysia. I recommended he try skydiving or paragliding and mentioned I was debating zorbing.

He mentioned an experience he had zorbing in Europe. The outfit they worked with had a unique zorbing setup. His friend went first and climbed inside a huge inflatable ball, which was also inside a larger inflatable ball. The larger ball goes rolling down the hill and you are in the very center of it. To me that sounded incredibly fun.

If nothing goes wrong.

During the never-ending sequence of flipping and being tossed about down a long grassy hill, his poor friend began vomiting and was not a pretty sight at the end. He emerged from the zorb covered in his own puke. It was right then and there I realized Queenstown would be phenomenal without zorbing or Fergburgers.

I met several hikers in Queenstown that were in the midst of trips around the world. I have never thought about taking one and was unaware so many people did until my travels of the past few years.

Very few people have the financial or logistical wherewithal to pull that off. I think the majority of earthlings wouldn't even enjoy such a trip.

Though it sounds exotic and adventurous, I know many people who truly love their vacations, but equally enjoy getting home from them. The very monotony of one's daily routine, that often makes a vacation sound incredible, can seem very inviting to return to.

I suppose many people like "the known" more than the randomness of being untethered to expectations or time schedules. Maybe we should differentiate between the groups: those who could travel endlessly and those who hug their mailbox upon return.

Maybe the term "vacationers" is befitting the tribe who loves getting back to the routine, while the term "travelers" better describes those who only come home because they have to.

Neither group is better than the other, there is no "right or wrong." It's simply personal preference. Like the example given at the beginning of the book, some people are wired to enjoy two weeks on the Amazon

River and would not consider a posh spa near a top bakery remotely enticing.

Yet, that spa and bakery overflow with people on a daily basis. There are countless types of people on Earth, and they all should seek whatever makes them happiest. I have numerous friends well into successful marriages who have very differing tastes in many things. Over the years, they realized they don't have to do those things together to be loyal, loving spouses.

They may take a vacation each year together, while also doing certain other things solo, or with friends with similar interests.

One of the "Around-the-World" travelers I met was a young lady from Sicily. We met atop a hill, with staggering views down onto Queenstown and Lake Wakatipu. She was traveling around the world alone. Her trip began eastward, and she had bounced around a couple stops in the Middle East, onward to India, then multiple stops in southeast Asia before landing in Australia and then to New Zealand.

After chatting for a while, we hiked together for a couple of hours. Eventually, I asked how this trip came to be: was a great life event driving the trip, sadness to escape, or maybe anger from a past experience?

She told the story of simply being bored with her career. Life wasn't unfolding the way she wanted it to. Not due to a lack of success, rather, the professional endeavors left her very unfulfilled.

She took a personal inventory of her life, her age (early 30s) and her ability to do something about it. Soon thereafter, she closed her small business, sold her possessions and hit the road. That trip would allow her plenty of time and perspective to decide what was next.

I asked her if she had felt safe traveling the world alone, and she said there was never a time she was worried. Clearly, on a planet of over seven billion people, there are millions of really bad people we all hope our lives avoid overlapping with.

We parted ways back in Queenstown as our accommodations were on opposite ends of town. She was packing that night and flying the next day to begin her next leg of the trip, bouncing around numerous countries in South America, starting in Chile.

I admired both her inspiration to change what she felt like was an uninspiring life and her moxie to do what most cannot conceive of.

Such a trip and life change may be far too unsettling for most people, but it was right for her and I applaud her for making the leap.

I took a tour from Queenstown down to Fjordland National Park to visit both Doubtful Sound and Milford Sound on different days. If incredible natural settings motivate you, these trips are worth every penny.

They aren't close enough to realistically visit both on the same day. Technically, they aren't sounds either; each is a fjord. When discussing the differences between fjords and sounds, you have to drag bays and bights into it. All of them are different but similar.

It is like to walking up to a pizza buffet. For many people, they don't need a description of each type. They all look good and they will have some of all of them. The particular eaters may want more info, but they aren't likely to be at a pizza buffet.

Visitors to Milford and Doubtful Sound will likely be in such awe of what they are seeing they won't care how the most diligent geographer classifies them. Taking a boat tour of each is the way to go. Our tour boat spent a couple of hours slowly probing the nooks and crannies.

It really felt like we were the first humans to see them. Milford Sound was first discovered by Europeans in the 1800s. That's not to say it was "discovered" then. Most of the English-speaking world has a strange focus on when Europeans discovered far-reaching places. This is even more odd considering that much of Europe wasn't English-speaking when they dominated world discovery.

To say Milford Sound was discovered in the 1800s ignores the indigenous Maori culture which knew of it over a millennium ago. Equally laughable is Columbus "discovering" America and meeting tribes. If he discovered it, how could there be civilizations already there.

I should walk into a gleaming shopping mall, plant a flag and claim to discover it.

Doubtful Sound was "first" spotted by English explorer Captain Cook. Though it is the deepest of the fjords in New Zealand, Cook couldn't have known that and chose to not explore it, being "doubtful" it was navigable.

Milford and Doubtful Sound feel mystical. Tall mountains surround the really dark water. Mist and shadows lend a sense of wonder. On the day I was at Milford Sound, we enjoyed bright sunshine for the majority of the day. Under the sun and blue skies, Milford Sound was stunning. New Zealand wisely incorporated these areas into a National Park to preserve the natural beauty and prevent development.

As the boat crawled about, there was no hint of human presence outside of those on the tour. It looked absolutely untouched and timeless. Cuba is often referred to as a "time warp" due to the lack of trade the island nation has had due to their political structure.

Moving about Havana, the old American cars from the 1950s, along with the decades old billboards, certainly gave that impression.

The areas within Fjordland National Park more closely resembled a time warp to me. It couldn't have looked any different centuries ago.

Many people I know are more impressed with the feats and innovations of humans, and I understand that allure. It is fascinating. On those tours of New Zealand's timeless, rugged nature, it wouldn't have seemed surprising if a massive Brontosaurus head suddenly emerged from the depths, towering over our tiny boat.

Despite being a herbivore, with no interest in munching humans, the people aboard would be in a massive panic, screaming and trampling each other. Predictably, some dunce with a selfie stick would want to get a picture with the plant-chewing monster.

Sadly, no dinosaurs emerged and placid waters remained calm. While on Doubtful Sound, we ran into some tough weather. Fog and mist enhanced the surroundings, but as the boat picked up speed, the wind began to whip.

New Zealand, particularly the South Island, really never gets "hot." This being November, we were in the late stages of spring, and the temps made jackets, hats and pants a wise choice.

As the tourists filled the belly of the boat, seeking peace from the elements, my desire to go out on the deck grew. There were food and drinks available inside. Many people seemed to prefer sitting there chatting. Engrossed in playing cards or discussing whatever, they rarely budged or even looked around at one of the most amazing places they would ever see.

Having been on the deck earlier before the wind picked up, I knew this was going to be incredibly raw. I opened a side door and stepped out. As I climbed the steps to the main deck, I had to lean forward with my head ducked.

The wind howled, making standing against the cabin wall a must to avoid being tossed about. I looked over at the few others also aboard the deck. I admired their willingness to get wind chapped in order to soak in the rare setting they may never see again. It likely made me feel less foolish to not be the only person up there.

One man, to my left, stood stoically. The wind caused his cheeks to flap like a Basset Hound with its head out the car window. I looked away and looked back several times. Human jowls flapping is not a desirable look. I struggled not to laugh.

Firmly in middle age, I realized I better check myself. Raising my hands to my cheeks and touching them lightly, I could feel a slight quivering of skin.

That is one of the inevitable parts of aging. The skin is no longer "high and tight" like a teenager's. Realizing I was morphing into "Basset Hound status" as well was a bit of a punch to the gut. There was no pity party though. Those of us on the deck took in the serenity for as long as we could stand it, leaving the comforts of the cabin to those who favor that.

During the tours of Milford and Doubtful Sound, penguins frolicked to the extent they can. Moving in a permanent waddle, everything penguins do tends to look the same. Seals are known to frequent the areas, particularly Doubtful Sound which is far bigger.

On the way back in, the boat cruised across a lake to get to the tour bus. The clouds parted, and the sun showcased as brilliant and impressive a rainbow as can exist. People flocked back onto the decks, taking video and pictures of the rainbow which looked like an artist's palette against the bright blue sky and dark blue water.

I would go back there with no hesitation but am glad to remember the first visit so vividly. It is the type of place that will always be more impressive on the first trip.

As my trip to New Zealand drew to a close, I took a tour of filming locations Hollywood has used in the area around Queenstown. The bulk of the locations were used in the filming of The Hobbit sequels.

As a kid, I drank in every word of Tolkien's epic books. At young ages, imaginations are powerful and active. As I read, the images came off of the pages. The setting seemed too good to be true—surreal. Where better to film those tales than the area around Queenstown.

For me, the Hobbit books are a great memory from elementary school. Four decades later, they don't interest me much. I took the tour forgetting that many adults have a ravenous interest in the characters and paraphernalia—literally everything associated with the books and films.

I was quickly reminded of that when I checked in at the tour office. To the rest of the people on the tour—all adults—I was a "non-believer." Several of them were wearing Hobbit hats, hoodies and the like. These people *loved* these novels. I was clearly out of my element but chose to play along.

Many years ago, my assistant wrestling coach Josh, was describing his dad's career in the railroad industry. He told of train fanatics that await the arrival of trains, not to pick up passengers but just to watch the "iron horse" arrive. To these people trains are a hobby they have great passion for.

His dad described these train lovers as "foamers," meaning they foam at the mouth when they see a train. I was on a tour with Hobbit "foamers." As we drove along Lake Wakatipu, one of the men became very animated, pointing and yelling, *"I remember this, I remember this!"* as he bounced around, utterly childlike.

I sat right behind him having no idea what he was talking about. He went on to describe the scene in detail to everyone. A couple of other tour members disputed his claims, and a full-fledged Hobbit ruckus broke out.

The poor tour guide couldn't get a word in, despite trying. Her utterances coming in a stream of one syllable grunts, "I..", "Th..", "Wh ...", "Th ...", "No ...", "But ..." hoping one of them would serve as a "pry bar" to insert herself into the conversation. I expected the foamers to collapse unconscious, from talking without breathing. Eventually they died down, and the guide spoke.

Foamer #1 was correct according to her. Some scene, from some movie, took place there and he recognized the setting! The backdrop! It wasn't even key to the scene and the guide said she was surprised he remembered it so well. At this point, I wished I was back on my endless drive through Oklahoma, being an outsider in a tumbleweed town for not driving a pickup.

Each stop along the tour elicited some arousal among the foamers. There were seven of us: three couples and myself. Among the others, two of the guys yammered on with excitement while their ladies mirrored my enthusiasm—feigning interest and checking our watches.

The third couple seemed to be equally inebriated by the tour. I'd say the girl likely foamed heavier. At one filming site, the guide broke out some snacks and provided conversation time. I asked her, away from the others, if she was a fan of the books and movies. She said her son was and she only watched the movies because of her job. She acknowledged enjoying the enthusiasm some tourists show for the series. I appreciated that.

Moments later, she offered us the opportunity to wear a cloak and hold a faux dagger, used in the filming, for photo opportunities. The foamers went bananas. Despite the distance, a Grand Canyon-like distance, between their love of this and mine, I was happy for them. It made for good people-watching.

I doubt two of the foamers washed the dagger-holding hand for weeks out of reverence for the props. When I politely declined my turn to wear the cloak and wield the dagger, one of them gasped. He took solace in having a second turn posing as a warrior from Middle-Earth.

We finished the tour, and my final evening in New Zealand drew near. I debated how to spend my final night in Queenstown. I did not want it to be hectic, nor could it be an "all evening" event due to the fact that I had to pack for an early flight the next day.

I decided to go to the one place I enjoyed the most—the Beach Bar Café. Neither hungry, nor thirsty, I still had a small sandwich and coffee, buying myself time to linger and enjoy a surreal sunset over Lake Wakatipu. I think the café is now a new restaurant. Regardless of whether the menu is nothing better than dogfood, the setting is worth the visit.

After sitting there for a couple of hours, I bought some bakery goods for my lodging hosts and began my final, one-mile walk back there. Lake Wakatipu tagged along on my left the entire way.

The owners of the house were a friendly, selfless couple who bought the house about 15 years earlier. What an investment it turned out to be. The view from their backyard is almost worth "foaming" over. The world has largely treasured Queenstown in the time since they purchased the house. They were so eager to make my stay as good as possible, and I appreciated their hospitality.

The next morning they insisted on giving me a ride to the airport. Sooner than I would have liked, Queenstown, and all of New Zealand, were a fresh memory. A great one. My flight to Auckland connected with another, eventually to land in Houston, then to St. Louis.

I was scheduled to land in St. Louis on the evening before the U.S. holiday of Thanksgiving. Due to the trip extending halfway around the globe and bounding through countless time zones, I had skipped an entire day of my life traveling to New Zealand. I left on a Wednesday, and 19 hours later, it was Friday.

The return trip would turn out to be a bit harrowing and the time schedule even quirkier.

When humans get a taste for something we tend to infuse that something into as many other somethings as we can. Bacon, for example, is ubiquitous now, and that is a good thing. There is no "look" to a bacon lover; I haven't met someone who doesn't enjoy it.

Chocolate is a lux food item we tend to find creative ways to enjoy as well.

I read somewhere that giving chocolate to the flight crew when boarding is a nice touch. Giving a gift is an obvious gesture of appreciation to people who typically get a smile and a "Thank You" at best. Despite recent bad PR for airlines involving passengers being removed from flights, many times the level of human stupidity flight crews have to deal with is cringe-worthy.

Most of my flights have involved harmless groups of travelers it seems, but with earbuds in, and shades on, how would I know? A flight departing Honolulu that was in the news once had to return to Hawaii because a drunkard was threatening people on board. Several times a month, passengers are in the news because they cannot "work and play well" with others.

On a leg of my New Zealand trip, the plane had to return to the gate so passengers flying under false IDs could be booted. How do I know that? The Power of Chocolate!

My flight to New Zealand seemed like the perfect opportunity. Lost in the midst of my own "How do I spend 14 hours on a plane?" pity party, was the reality that the flight crew may have a worse plight.

While prepping for the trip, I missed numerous chances to buy the chocolate, ultimately needing to do what I dread the most: *buy things at the airport.*

Dropping a mortgage in an airport store, I bought a bunch of Lady Godiva bars for the flight crew as we left San Francisco flying to Auckland. I handed the bars to one flight attendant as I stepped onto the plane and simply said, "Thank you in advance. Your crew has a long night ahead of you." The attendant was speechless, mouthing several things silently before saying, "Oh...... thank you so much!"

On the return trip from Auckland to Houston, I did the same thing. In the early stages of the flight, six or seven flight attendants came to my seat asking, "Are you the kind gentlemen that brought us chocolate?" Then, one at a time, they bestowed gifts upon me.

These items were things available on the plane, like pillows, blankets and headphones. Fortunately, there was an open seat to my right where all of this was heaped. The friendly couple on the other side of the pile of riches noticed curiously until finally I explained the unrealized "chocolate for airplane booty" trade agreement.

This flight would raise an issue I had never thought about previously. Flying through the night seems like a good idea. Any stretch of sleep would seem to shorten the flight—a very good thing when flying across an ocean.

As we settled in, lights were dimmed, chit chat died off and the majority of the passengers turned to headphones for entertainment. The couple to my right had been extremely friendly, and we both enjoyed the open seat, particularly on a long flight.

Evening merged into night, and I was awakened by several flight attendants. My being awakened was accidental. Their flashlights betrayed the hushed tones in which they spoke. The lady to my right was suffering some kind of medical problem.

She had fallen asleep leaning against her husband, who, at some point, tried to waken her and couldn't. She was breathing but unresponsive. The flight crew handled it deftly, realizing the sleeping passengers around us were best left to sleep. A passenger onboard was a doctor, and she was summoned to our row.

I later asked a flight attendant how they knew she was a doctor, or that there was even a doctor onboard. She told me people with medical training often make that known when traveling. Somehow, I never knew that, though topics I know nothing about are as numerous as tween girls at a "boy band" concert.

I gave up my seat to allow the doctor space. It was astonishing how fast the ill passenger took a turn for the worse. I nodded toward her husband, and a flight attendant took me to the very back row of the plane which was totally empty.

Sleep and I were done with one another for the night. I plugged in and watched a fairly good movie. I was so far away from my original seat, and the medical crisis, that I could not even see the people attending to her. I looked at the flight map on the screen in front of me to see where we were, figuring we may have to make an unplanned stop in Hawaii to get her to a hospital.

I had forgotten that the flight path to Houston from so deep in the southern hemisphere would come nowhere close to Hawaii. In fact, we were nowhere close to anything. The next country with medical facilities was likely Chile or Ecuador in South America, both of which were hours away.

Medical disasters happen every day with absolutely no notice. Many traffic accidents are actually caused by the driver being stricken with a medical emergency prior to the crash.

Airplanes fly across oceans hundreds of times a day, yet I had never thought about how such situations are handled. It speaks to the training the flight crews must have that is invisible to passengers because such crises rarely arise.

A couple of hours later, I asked one of the flight attendants how the lady was doing. She replied very casually that she was doing much better.

A few more hours went by and passengers began to mumble and chat. Windows were opened to let the sunshine through, and epically long lines formed near the restrooms. With about an hour left in the flight, a crew member came to me and said I was welcome to return to my original seat if I wanted. Being so much farther forward in the plane, I would exit much quicker if I chose to return.

Surprised they no longer needed the entire row for the sick passenger, I asked for an update. They replied she was totally fine. That shocked me. I was thrilled for them but wondered how someone can be unresponsive at 2am and completely fine just six hours later. They mentioned dehydration, fluids and things along those lines.

I gathered my things and returned to my seat for a reunion with the couple. She smiled and thanked me for my concern, apologizing for the hassle. I told her it was no problem at all and explained that, instead of celebrating a single open seat, her incident landed me in an *entire row* to myself. She smiled and laughed.

I could not have been happier that she was fine. A great trip ended on a very upbeat note. A great American holiday was waiting, and my friend from the flight was feeling great. The time zone hopping should have hammered me with intense jetlag, but it never really happened.

The time zones did create a very weird circumstance. As I walked off of the plane to fetch my suitcase, it was technically two hours before I even boarded it. My flight left on a Wednesday evening, and 14 hours later, landed two hours earlier than it left.

There has to be a way to make money doing that.

This epic trip was my final one of 2016. Having visited Cuba in January and Canada in July, this was a year my life would pivot on.

My 25-year career teaching history had ended in May. An early retirement package was, like nachos after a hike, too strong to resist. Likewise, my career in high school coaching would end a few months later.

After 36 seasons as a head coach of three sports, people would no longer call me "Coach." I loved that title but needed a change.

This trip was the tonic I needed. It was an adventure that gave me plenty of time to think. I was living through a period of deep sadness at the time. A short but incredible relationship ended very poorly for me. Losing her cut deep.

The bulk of my sadness rotated around how it all happened, how she handled the situation. Finding out she eventually married was like digging a knuckle into a severe bruise.

Guys are infamous for internalizing things. Many people I know well never knew about the depth of the sadness. Immediately after the relationship ended, I passed up social offers. Being home sounded better. Television was the babysitter, but my attention was focused on a blank spot on a wall.

Eventually, I stared at that wall long enough, it could have gotten a restraining order against me. I was able to see the situation for what it was: something with no cure. Time would heal it. Each day nudged me closer to seeing "mental sunshine" again, but only a millimeter at a time.

I wished her well and tried to forgive. I want to be the person that can do that, but I spent more time marinating in misery. Along the way, I dated, hoping to meet the person that could banish all moping. Perhaps I did, but the timing was obviously awful and nothing could possibly have taken root.

It was on those three trips that I felt happiest. Being distracted by phenomenal sights, foods and people-watching began to vault me back amongst those "living" life. Months later I started to feel like myself again. The slog of sadness and misery was over.

Jumping out of airplanes and running off of cliffs will slap a guy out of ruminating over just about anything.

Freed up from career obligations, I had nothing preventing me from doing *exactly* what I wanted to do as a second career. I knew what that was and worked toward it.

But first, I sat in a pub built by Vikings and saw what might possibly be the biggest biker ever known to roam the earth on a trip to Ireland.

CHAPTER 7 - IRELAND

The Emerald Isle had been on my list a very long time. Dublin, and Ireland in general, are generally perceived as a charming part of the "Old World." Reputed to have an epic pub life and very friendly people, it sounded like the perfect landing spot for a summer trip.

My friend, Mark, found a trip through a tour company he really respects. We debated whether to go it alone, making our own plans, allowing for last minute whims, but eventually chose to sign up for a "Food and Drink Tour."

The title alone made it sound like a great idea. Ireland is certainly not considered a "Foodie Destination" in the culinary world, like France or Italy, but there are great restaurants everywhere, as we would soon find out.

We arrived at the airport in St. Louis, fired up for an 11-day trip. As the passengers gathered at the gates, an interesting opportunity arose. The gate agent announced that the flight was overbooked and they needed two passengers to give up their seats so members of their crew could arrive in Chicago for their next flight.

The "enticing" part of the offer was vouchers worth $400 per passenger. My ears perked up like a Chihuahua. Vouchers are like free money, and who doesn't like free money? I glanced to Mark and asked the question without saying a word. Having made reservations through a travel tour company, rearranging flights and times wasn't as easy as us simply wanting to. We were arriving in Dublin two and a half days before the tour began. There was wiggle room, but the voucher had to be worth the hassle.

I looked around for people interested in the offer. No one budged. Many didn't even appear to have heard the announcement. Many travelers flying from Saint Louis to Chicago are doing so for business and lack the flexibility required, even if they're interested.

About 15 minutes later, the agent made the same announcement, but upped the ante by offering vouchers worth $600 per passenger. Again, I scouted the area; no one blinked. Mark and I discussed it very little but were getting closer to pulling the trigger on the deal. As boarding time drew near, the situation got a little more tense for the agent. If no passengers willingly gave up their seats, names are generated from a computer, and two unlucky souls are told they won't be flying.

You can imagine the ruckus this might cause if it happened to someone from the "Happy $%#$!!! Birthday" crew.

She made the announcement two more times, bumping the offer up each time to $800 and then $1,000 in vouchers per passenger. I was now rubbing my head, aware I was morphing into a "voucher foamer." Mark walked off to call the tour company and alert them to our change in plans. While I strolled over to the desk to close the deal, the agent made another request, upping the offer to $1200 in vouchers per passenger.

No longer caring if any other passengers budged, I told her we could give up our seats, and she was extraordinarily thankful. She had already been given the "green light" to offer $1400 per person, and though she hadn't announced that yet, she told me she would give us that amount. There was full-blown "voucher foaming." I almost needed a bib.

I was already mentally buying plane tickets with those vouchers. The adjustment in our schedule would delay our arrival in Dublin about 10 hours. I would be getting paid handsomely to go home, take a nap and come back later—an arrangement I would often do for free.

Suddenly, a bunch of airline employees, presumably the crew they were trying to stash on the plane, arrived at the desk, chatted, then walked off. The agent waved me over, thanked me and then said they no longer needed the two seats. The staff had made other arrangements to get to Chicago.

A verbal kick to the crotch.

Smiling on the outside, and stomping my feet on the inside, I looked at her blankly. I told her I understood and walked away. As with many things in life, what you see as bad news upfront often turns out best in the long run. We boarded the plane and flew to Chicago.

We had a two-hour layover in Chicago before connecting to Dublin. O'Hare Airport likely has more shops and stores than two thirds of the towns in America. Finding something to do would be no problem—a guy can always eat.

We found seats at a restaurant and ordered a flatbread pizza. It cost $13, didn't taste very good and was only slightly larger than a hockey puck. We didn't mind the small portion. We were going to have stretch marks after the "Food and Drink Tour" as it was. The price and quality bothered us a little more.

We settled in at the gate, waiting to board and saw something new to both of us. Traveling to Dublin with us was a group of a dozen or so Hells Angels. Bikers are just people, so it is logical they would travel. I've just never seen them do it outside of a highway.

The Hells Angels waiting at the gate were a diverse group. Ranging in age from mid 20s to around 70, they also represented nearly every body type. This crew provided the bulk of the denim, bandannas and tattoos in the area. The one thing they all had in common was the Hells Angels jacket.

Surprising to me, two of the younger bikers had skateboards as carry-ons. Skateboarders and Hells Angels never meshed in my mind. I have no problem with skateboarders. They are fearless and many are freakishly talented. I just saw them being an entirely different group of people from the biker world.

I always imagined biker gangs seeing a kid on a skateboard, laughing and grunting while running him off the road. The deep grumbles of their bike engines disturbing the peace as the skateboarder lay concussed at the base of a light pole. Add biker gangs to the list of things I know nothing about.

A Hells Angel then stood up, coming in to view for the first time. He was absolutely *enormous*! He was the tallest guy in the gate area and positively jacked from an enormous commitment to the weight room.

He wore a sleeveless shirt, exposing massive arms bulging like cannon balls. If I had arms like that, I wouldn't even *own* a pair of sleeves.

Sleeveless tuxedo? Yep. Sleeveless suit? You got it.

He looked like he should emerge from the sea and start stomping Tokyo to dust while breathing fire at whatever he chose. It looked like he could choke a giraffe to death with one hand, while flinging a rhinoceros about with the other.

I am rarely the biggest guy in a crowd but always one of the biggest. I couldn't help but think several steps ahead of the situation. Amateur wrestlers stand a better than average chance against nearly anyone. Creating a bunch of "What if" scenarios in my head, I tried to figure out a way that I could physically deal with this guy if I needed to. Unless I could find a slingshot and a rock, my best plan was hoping I could injure his fists with my face.

To represent them fairly, the Hells Angels stuck to themselves, didn't draw attention and blended in as well as a biker gang can—except the gargantuan biker, who could not blend in anywhere.

We boarded the plane and seemingly waited forever. We spent nearly two hours just sitting there. Something was up. Eventually, the pilot left the cockpit and walked to two men seated about 10 rows in front of me. Those men exited the plane, and immediately afterward, we were in the air. The delay was directly related to those two men.

Later in the flight, a lady walked to the back of plane and stood near my seat waiting for the bathroom. I asked her if she knew what caused the delay, or why those guys left the plane. She told me she was seated across the aisle from them. One of them was acting completely normal, but his friend was behaving erratically.

Her career involves working with drug addicts in recovery. She said she had no doubt drugs were the cause of his state and that it looked like he was hallucinating. As he began drawing attention, a couple of the Hells Angels seated nearby told him to get his act together; they weren't putting up with that stuff.

The way she described the interaction, the bikers weren't out of line, they were just hoping to prevent a problem that could arise on an eight-hour flight with someone clearly under the influence of something.

We arrived in Dublin at about 8am, and, surprisingly, were able to check in at the hotel at that early hour. Realistically, we each slept for only a couple of hours on the overnight flight and we were starting to feel it.

When traveling east through multiple time zones, the recommended way of minimizing jet lag is to simply stay awake until the locals hit the sack. Doing this helps adjust one's body clock to the daily routines and times of the place you are in.

We planned to walk all over Dublin that day. Irish weather is known to be finicky, but on this day, we were lucky. It was sunny and in the 60s F (17 C)—perfect for a long day of walking and gawking.

Arriving at the tail end of the morning rush in a city the size of Dublin, traffic in the downtown area was predictably heavy. After walking about for a couple of hours, I noticed how many people commuted to and fro on bicycles.

They were not cruising in designated bike lanes. They were in the midst of the cars, pedaling fast and changing lanes just like cars would. I was impressed how deftly they use hand signals to communicate with drivers near them while maintaining their focus forward as they desperately needed to.

I was genuinely amazed at their comfort on a bike surrounded by cars and how well they blended into the traffic pattern. Clearly, they have a lot of experience with this, as did the drivers around them. I've spent a lot of time on a bike in my life, and I assure you there would be major problems if I tried to do this.

When I was a kid, I was lucky to live in a neighborhood full of other kids. We had the idyllic childhood in that way. In the middle of our neighborhood there was a very small city block that had only about 10 houses on its rectangular perimeter.

The other boys and I would race each other on bikes around this block, kind of equivalent to sprinting one lap on a track. In hindsight, it's amazing at least one of us didn't end up as goo on the front of an oncoming car—like a big bug splattered on a windshield. We peddled like crazy, and despite leaning into the turn, would swing wide, not knowing what may be coming in the other direction.

One day, when I was about eight years old, my parents left for the day, leaving my older sister and aunt in charge. My sister was just one grade above me and my aunt was a young teenager.

This was an era when kids commonly drank from hoses, lived with lead paint, rode in cars with no seat belts and didn't even know what bike helmets were.

Health food wasn't promoted, and one of the medicines we used for daily scrapes and cuts was Mercurochrome, which the FDA unofficially banned a couple of decades later by requiring testing that no one chose to do.

We would leave the house early in the day having no idea where we were going to end up. Cell phones didn't exist, so parents more or less just hoped we made it home alive at the end of the day. It was incredible.

My bike was black with tall handlebars, a banana seat with a racing flag standing tall off of the back of the frame. It ripped and swayed in the wind on our various forays into strange, unexplored neighborhoods. Before trying to round up friends, I wanted to take a hard lap on the bike.

I decided to count, "one Mississippi, two Mississippi" style, while pedaling, to arrive at my finish time. Incredibly unscientific, and equally inaccurate, that logic describes the thought process of a third grader.

I started pedaling at the beginning of a long stretch of the street. Standing up on the pedals, and cranking furiously, I headed into the first turn feeling like a pro. Swinging far wider then I safely should, I was lucky the street was empty. This stretch of the block was very short, I could only stand on the pedals and hammer out some more speed for maybe 10 seconds before having to stop pedaling and lean into the next turn.

The way the houses sat on this corner, I could see what was in the road ahead after the second turn. A few parked cars would be easy to avoid. The street was all mine.

A few months earlier, one of the kids I hung out with daily had a spectacular bike wreck. His small dog had gotten out and bolted down the street. My friend, Ron and I were already on our bikes and pursued the fur ball that was still scampering across some front yards.

My friend was pedaling down the edge of the street, looking to his left and calling out to his dog, hoping it would stop. I was on his right, on my bike, doing the same thing. Neither of us were looking ahead. Suddenly there was a loud crashing sound that immediately jerked my attention toward it. Ron had ridden his bike right into the front of a parked car that he never saw.

I watched him soar over his handlebars and onto the hood of the car. He slid up the windshield and back down it in a jumbled heap. A scary pause of several seconds, just silence, seemed to stretch far longer.

I stood straddling my bike in the middle of the street, scared and astonished. Mouth open, eyes wide, possibly looking at my first dead person. Suddenly he sprang to life, crawled off of the car, and sprinted into his house screaming and crying.

I had seen Ron bleed, take basketballs right to the face, and fall at a full sprint, but had never seen him cry before. Stunned, I knew this meant he was probably hurt, maybe badly. I was still in the street frozen as a car crept up behind me.

The driver likely had no idea why a twerp was standing in the middle of the road looking like he just saw a monster. His "honk" was intended to just alert me, but given what just happened, I may have peed a little.

Forgetting I was standing over a bike, I flailed about trying to run out of the way. I stumbled embarrassingly as legs and bike kept crashing into one another in my panic to get out of the way. Eventually, dragging my bike off of the road as though it were unconscious, the car drove by, and I saw the driver chuckling. Ron survived relatively unscathed, aside from a broken arm.

As I flew around the second turn on my glory ride, I stood on the pedals again to power up even more speed. I noticed the same car Ron hit, parked in the exact same spot. I smirked that the car would not get me. I was past halfway on the loop. All I had to do was accelerate into this final turn and then power up a steep but short hill. Whatever my "time" would be, it would set a record in my mind.

I churned downward on the pedals, as though punishing them, and something really strange, and bad, happened.

My front wheel wobbled. Then it fell completely off.

The forks of my black bike dug into the pavement, and I was launched over the handlebars and flung forward. My face, right shoulder and arm took the brunt of the impact, with my feet hanging above my head like a scorpion's tail. I skidded painfully to a stop right at the base of a mailbox. This crash site was a baseball throw from my house, just around the corner and out of sight.

The arrival of pain and tears was quick. I cried, lying in the street, likely more scared than hurt. The owner of that mailbox came out of the house and walked right toward me. I was at least glad help was on the way.

As he got to me, he glanced down at me as though I was yesterday's morning paper, stepped over me, grabbed his mail and walked back in the house. I vowed in that moment to someday toilet paper his yard like no one had ever toilet-papered a yard.

That caused anger and more tears. I stood and shuffled up the hill like an extra in a zombie movie. As I got to the edge of my front yard, my aunt and older sister rushed out to see what was wrong. Upon seeing me, they ran back into the house to get what was needed. I was a mess.

Having skidded on pavement, the damage was mostly road rash. Huge amounts of my right forearm, shoulder and side of my face would someday be scabs. For now, they were just raw and filthy. *M-a-n,* did it hurt.

As I staggered into the house, my sister and aunt sat me down and did their best. They doused huge wads of paper towels with peroxide, then slapped those soaked wads onto the road rash, eliciting another round of shocking pain. Based on the screams, the neighbors may have thought a beaver was chewing my leg off.

Though awful to look at, the wounds were superficial. I was a kid of the 1970s. I survived.

Arriving home later, my dad fetched the carcass of my bike from the road near the mailbox. A couple of days later, a neighbor from the bottom of the hill walked up to the house carrying a front wheel from a bike he found in his yard. He had heard about the wreck and knew where to bring it.

That memory pulsed as I watched these cyclists immersed in Dublin's traffic. I asked a cabbie if there were many accidents involving cars and bikes, noting how impressed I was with their two-wheeled bravado. He cringed and said that there are, including a fatal one just a week earlier.

I think it is best I don't join that urban mosh pit of vehicles on a bike.

Jet lag is more powerful than I knew. I had more or less been spared of its impact during my previous travels. We sat down at a burger joint called Eddie Rockets overlooking the River Liffey. By now, the jet lag was winning. During the few minutes we sat after finishing the burgers, literally nothing on Earth sounded better than just sleeping.

As Mark talked, I sat facing him. My sunglasses hid the fact my eyes were shut. Seated outside in perfect temps, a slight breeze had a "sandman" effect. It felt sooooooo good to just close my eyes. I managed to sit in such a way that my head wouldn't bob downward, betraying my attempt to steal 20 winks while feigning listening carefully.

I woke up to, *"Are you sleeping?"*—another question not needing an answer. I laughed and we got up to trudge through the city. We headed toward Dublin's oldest pub, The Brazen Head, which dates back to the year 1198.

Think about how long ago that was.

Christopher Columbus was over 200 years from being born and George Washington didn't arrive for over 500 years. This was the era where armies still used catapults to lob boulders at the walls of enemy forts, sometimes squashing some unlucky soldiers when boulders accidentally cleared the fortress wall.

Cannons didn't exist in Europe yet. This was the "Knight in Shining Armor" era. And w-a-a-a-a-y back then in the Viking settlement today called Dublin, a pub was built and is still open today.

Though I enjoyed my burger (and nap) earlier, we should have eaten at The Brazen Head. It has the design typical of that era: a lot of small rooms and a low ceiling. Finding the bathroom was like walking a labyrinth.

In the Viking era, a thousand years ago to simplify the math, mainland Europe shuddered at the mention of the "Northmen" or "Norseman" who occasionally would arrive. These Vikings would pillage, take supplies and wealth and leave battered opponents. They then boarded their boats with dragon head carvings affixed to the front, and headed back to Scandinavia.

The word "berserk" comes from the maniacal frenzy that elite Viking warriors, "berzerkers," fought with. Some historians believe this may have been drug or alcohol induced. These crazed men are said to have fought in a trance-like state, often fighting naked under an animal skin tunic of sorts.

Fighting a Viking warrior in battle was an absolute nightmare for soldiers throughout Europe. Being so very unfortunate to encounter a "berzerker" simply meant you were going to die and possibly have your body shred to bits.

Mark enjoyed a pint, and I downed a cider as we looked around a building built by Vikings. We joked that we were sitting in a spot where the world's nuttiest warriors once sat. Big, burly bearded men would drink and discuss the beatings they dispensed on the rest of Europe.

And this was their pub.

By that evening, we had walked over ten miles. The combination of fatigue from a long walk, and feeling completely drunk from a lack of sleep, left us both daffy beyond description. Credit goes to Mark, who manag-ed to navigate our way around Dublin despite his mental fog. I was so tired, operating a toilet was about as ambitious an endeavor as I could manage.

Eating dinner, we went through the motions—chomping and chewing while not remotely enjoying it. We had one thing left to do at the hotel before face planting and lying motionless for hours.

There are 16 pubs in Dublin that have been open since the Victorian era in the 1800s. We were going to hit all 16 of them the next day. That required a lot of planning, including coordinating various forms of public transit and plotting the order of the pubs on a map to minimize wasted time.

All of that planning awaited us at a time when our IQs were halved by delirium, and we had less focus than a teenage boy trying to study inside a yoga class.

Weaving through the streets of Dublin, we managed to find the hotel and got right to work. At this point, I was intermittently laughing in random bursts for no apparent reason. Everything was funny just because we were so tired.

Mark was doing the planning, and I was writing down the order on a legal pad while giggling and laughing. It was a list of 16 pubs with notes in the margin detailing the most logical travel arrangements from one pub to the next. After finishing number 15, I managed to fall asleep in the tiny fraction of a second that exists between writing 1 and 6. Slap happy once again, this set off a bout of laughter and crying.

For our schedule to work the next day, we needed to be at the first pub that opened at 10:30am. It was not close by so we needed to leave the hotel at about 9:30. It was 8pm and the sun was still up. From across the room, Mark asked if we should set an alarm. I told him no alarm was needed.

I only sleep a maximum of six or seven hours at a time. I would be up no later than 5am whether I wanted to be or not. We finished the list and immediately crashed.

We woke up to the maid knocking. It was a few minutes shy of 14 hours later, and we were already 15 minutes behind schedule. I had not moved from the position in which I fell asleep.

Our plan from the night before was already scuttled, but the mood was so good, we were unfazed and would adjust on-the-fly. We headed out as soon as we were cleaned up. The great weather of the day before was gone. This was a gray misty day, very common on the small island in the Atlantic Ocean. Foot traffic on the streets was as heavy as the day before. Daredevil cyclists still flowed among vehicles.

To Dubliners, this was just another day. On a bus we chatted with some ladies from New York. They were on a much longer trip that would take them to France and Italy before they headed home. I enjoyed how excited they were and imagined the fun they would have on the rest of the trip.

We got to our stop, exited, and walked to the first pub on the list. As the rain picked up, Mark asked me for his umbrella which I carried on the bus. Intending to put it in my backpack, I didn't because it was wet. I'm sure whoever found it lying on the bus floor later that day made good use of it since I had forgotten it. Ball caps and hoods would have to be good enough.

To make the tour legitimate, we agreed that we would have to order something in each pub. We alternated who ordered the drink to slow the process and maintain our wits. Having learned the hard way, I prefer feeling great first thing in the morning rather than at 10pm.

To many people who visit Dublin, maintaining one's sobriety is a ridiculous thought. More power to them. We ran into plenty like them in the pubs, particularly in the evening as people arrived from work. They cackled and swayed, puppets to the effects of Guinness.

Some of the pubs were very small and in bad parts of town while others were large, lively and located in gentrified areas. In each, you were sure to see locals at the bar with a pint of Guinness sitting in front of them. The dark pint with the creamy white froth at the top seemed to be part of the uniform of a Dublin native.

Every local we spoke to was extraordinarily friendly, with the exception of one bartender who had the people skills of a Great White Shark. Everyone else chatted freely, offering the history that they knew the respective building to have.

In one pub, I noticed some bottles sitting atop a cabinet by the bar. The labels and glass looked very old. They were perched in a place much easier for a customer to see than the bar staff. I asked the bartender how old those bottles were, pointing up to them.

She expressed surprise to see them. She did not even know they were there. A young worker climbed up and retrieved one of the bottles. The label indicated the bottle was from the first decade of the 1900s. That was typical of the bars on the list. They looked old in a legitimate way. Not trashy, but distinguished. People that love architecture (and alcohol) would love to visit these pubs. Most were noteworthy with old handcrafted dark wood behind the bar and conversations at each table: some rollicking, others more private.

In all, it took us over nine hours to complete the tour and was another walking day of over ten miles, which was fine with us.

As one would expect, some pubs had younger more vibrant crowds while others are frequented by older regulars. The order we followed is below, along with the exact notes from that day. The attention span waned at times. I highly recommend doing this tour if you visit Dublin. If all 16 sounds too daunting, research and visit the eight oldest. Keep in mind that weekdays and evenings will be less lively than weekends which may make it more or less attractive. My only advice? Set an alarm.

1. Dublin Pub Tour Game Plan (along with incomplete thoughts and notes as taken during the tour).

2. Slatterlys Bar – Walked to . . ., Tram a great option as we walked along the tracks the entire way.

3. Ryan's Steakhouse

4. The Hut – friendly staff, dude at Trinity College.

5. Gaffney's and Sons pub – Dark, multiple rooms, friendly locals.

6. Finnegans Michelle Obama drank here, also frequented by Bono of U2. Via dart to Tara Street.

7. Bowe's Lounge – cool –

8. The Palace bar – nice –

9. The Norseman – opened in 1696, oldest bar in the Temple Bar area. Got there after work hours. Live music, great energy.

10. Staggs Head –

11. International bar

12. Kehoe's bar cool – lively.

13. Long Haul –

14. Swan bar – 1667- interior dates to 1897. Very cool, not lively at 8:45 pm Wednesday

15. Cassidy's Bar

16. Dogeny & Nesbitt (pronounced Donny). Cool place/ friendly help.

17. Toners

The gluttony of a food and drink tour is extreme. To sign up for such a tour and then complain about all of the food and drinks may indicate a genetic link to members of the dreaded "Happy %$#%$$!!! Birthday" crowd. Or worse, someone claiming their luggage is being held hostage.

In fairness, we did not hear any other members of the tour group complaining about the abundance of food and drinks on a tour designed around food and drinks. The tour was tastefully done in every way.

I went there more to see Ireland than to overindulge. After a few days, food got less and less enjoyable, and the post-meal misery got worse and worse. Walking around uncomfortably stuffed, I vowed to eat very little the next day, resolute in those plans until food was put in front of me.

Every bit of this was my fault, yet I would repeat the same cycle the next day. One day late in the week, I went for a run in the quaint harbor town of Kinsale, in southwestern Ireland. It is one of my favorite places to have visited anywhere in the world.

Very narrow streets and old stone buildings gave it a definite medieval charm. It reminded me of how I hear coastal Maine described, or the setting of a Christmas movie—a place too charming to be real.

I hoped to run for 30 minutes and push the pace in an attempt to undo some of the caloric carnage. I had to settle for 20 minutes of brutally slow running. I felt like a sumo wrestler and smelled like halibut and asparagus. Proud to have been an athlete with some measure of success, I couldn't stand the feeling of a waddling through town like an overfed penguin.

Upon returning from the trip, the scale confirmed my suspicions—five pounds gained in eleven days.

Kinsale, Ireland, sits at the mouth of the River Bandon. On a hill across the harbor from our hotel was a centuries old pub called The Spaniard. It is built on the remains of an old castle and is frequently mentioned in books, lists and articles touting things to do or places to go before you die.

Sitting on a hillside, it is easy to see due to the eye-catching yellow paint. After yet another phenomenal meal, Mark and I visited The Spaniard. It reeks of charm in the old-world style. Much like The Brazen Head, it is made up of small rooms, low ceilings and skinny doors.

Seated outside, a low stone wall ran the length of the narrow patio. You could feel the history in this place. Having spent a week together already, Mark and I were bored beyond words with one another's company. We struck up a conversation with two ladies who hailed from Budapest, Hungary. In fact, one was from Buda, and the other from Pest. The Hungarian capital city was formed when Buda and Pest consolidated. Ireland has had a big influx of Eastern Europeans over the past couple of decades. These two ladies, from the same capital city elsewhere in Europe, actually met one another in Ireland.

They were a lot of fun and quick to laugh. They lived in Cork, a city we visited briefly, and a place I would love to spend a lot more time. They regaled us with their thoughts on Ireland and Hungary. Time flew by, and we moved inside to escape the dropping temperatures.

Eventually, sophomoric games broke out. Flipping and trying to catch coasters, trying to toss peanuts in each other's mouths and all kinds of relaxed fun. Eventually we said our goodbyes, knowing we would never see them again. We stay in touch a bit through social media. That night will stand as so many other travel experiences do—an opportunity to chat and laugh with people from far away countries and make friends in distant parts of the world.

As Mark and I walked down the hill, looping left around the harbor, we noticed a boat sitting on the ground, leaning sideways. The darkness did not help clarify the situation. The two of us stood there puzzled for a bit.

Eventually though, it dawned on us that the entire harbor had emptied due to low tide. The few boats moored there sat awkwardly on the muddy ground waiting for the waters to return. In Missouri where I grew up, there is never a lack of water. Due to St. Louis sitting at the confluence of two major rivers, The Missouri and Mississippi, flooding on a small or large scale is quite often a problem.

Seeing a body of water completely disappear, return and disappear again, in a constant cycle, was fascinating. How and why that happens is well beyond my IQ. What is normal to some people is new and interesting to others—another reason to book a trip.

The city of Dublin was well worth the stay. For some travelers, the Irish capital city alone would be well worth the trip. Trinity College was a fascinating place. It too predates the U.S. by more than a century. The library on campus has a 500-year-old Bible in it.

Hailing from a country not even 300 years old, it was good to visit a far older city.

We all know that mountains and beaches preexisted any human civilization. A book that is older than the United States has a different impact. It serves as tangible proof that a civilization not only existed, but thrived, in one part of the world, while in another, indigenous peoples lived more primitive, yet still noble lives.

Due to various disputes in England in the early 1700s, Catholics were banned from the throne. Eventually, the throne of Britain passed to a distant heir, George I, who happened to live in Germany.

George I was both far, far down the pecking order to take the throne and the highest-ranking Protestant. So a German man, one many historians believe didn't even speak English, became the King of England. A time of three consecutive King Georges, known as the "Georgian Era," ensued.

The various eras of architecture were interesting to take in. Much of what people refer to as a "colonial architecture" jives with that of the Georgian era. It is a blessing the architecture could keep people's attention back then. The Georgian era is not a high spot in the history of human hygiene. Bathing was something people got around to once in a while. Washing the hands, feet and face happened on close to a daily basis, but scrubbing the rest of the body happened more or less once a month.

Women of the era were known for their long straight hair which was typically washed once a month at the most. A lot of bathing was simply submerging oneself in lakes, rivers and oceans, nude most of time, which made a "day at the beach" an entirely different experience.

The stink cloud drifting in and around Dublin, and all of Europe, in that day wasn't entirely due to body odor. The toothbrush, as we know it, didn't exist until the 1930s. Though people had tried various ways to keep their teeth clean for thousands of years, nothing really worked all that well—one reason paintings from centuries past rarely show anyone smiling.

They did the best they could with limited medical knowledge. For a time, people used sticks and twigs to try to remove food from their teeth. There was a belief in parts of Europe that one's own urine was the best way to keep teeth clean. In parts of Europe, gunpowder was even suggested as a method, one hopefully used while sober. I reminded myself, while taking in the old-world architecture, at least I had the opportunity to do so without enduring the stench of everyone around me, or my own personal funk.

Or kissing someone that rinsed their mouth with urine.

The Cliffs of Moher are a fabulous spectacle. Standing atop them and watching the Atlantic Ocean crash onto the rocks below was mesmerizing. We were, again, fortunate to have good weather for walking about clifftops and gawking at one of Earth's natural wonders.

As is the case near every spectacular sight, there was a big visitor center, with bathrooms, food options, hordes of tourists and enough souvenir trinkets to fill the Grand Canyon. The drive from Dublin was a six-hour round-trip, which I did not see as a deterrent. I wanted to visit the Irish countryside, and it did not disappoint.

Sunny skies illuminated numerous shades of green, the white of sheep shone brightly in contrast. Gray rock walls made of field stones lined the boundaries of pastures. This scene was continuous across Ireland, broken up only by the occasional small town.

Atop the Cliffs of Moher, the tourist throng spread along the vast expanse of the Cliffs. Yellow ropes indicated where it was recommended to stand. Many, including myself, walked to the very edge. The experience at peering down to the surf was worth the risk of land giving way under me. Seeing birds rise without flapping their wings, due to the updraft of winds off of the cliff, added to the uniqueness.

The World Surfing Championships have been, and again will be, held in the waters just south of the Cliffs of Moher. All I know about surfing is that I cannot do it. World class surfers, enormously talented, have to be a mentally-unique breed simply to be willing to co-mingle with sharks and the like.

The winds across the Atlantic can cause enormous waves. Ireland's location makes it something of a bodyguard for Great Britain, taking the wrath of these storms. Winds and waves *pound* the Irish coast, creating the type of areas small boats prefer to avoid, but surfers love.

When first told they would be competing in the frigid waters off the Irish coast, even a famously laid-back group like surfers had to raise an eyebrow. These waters are *c-o-l-d*. The typical beachgoer visiting these sands would dip a toe in the water, scream and sprint to the car never to come back.

When the Titanic sank, it was the frigid water temperatures that took many lives. The beaches holding these surfing championships are on a similar latitude, just a bit north of where the Titanic sank.

Wetsuits can only do so much. If there were any doubt surfers are a tough breed, surfing the coast of Ireland should remove it.

A U.S. customs agent, who processed my departure while still in Ireland, weighed in on the weather there. When asked how he liked living in Ireland, he said he loved it; the quaint towns and Irish people were great, but he could not wait to leave. He goes home to the U.S. every chance he gets, just due to the wind and temperatures. People from colder climates would likely be nonplussed by the fickle weather, but it certainly doesn't remind one of surfing.

The rest of the trip was focused in southwestern Ireland, bouncing around quaint towns like Kilarney, Cork and Kinsale with yet more food and drink. Having already visited the Jamison and Guinness plants, we visited yet another, far smaller microbrewery. All three were interesting, but having visited major breweries in the states, it lacked "first layer" intrigue, similar to re-reading a good book.

If I had control of the itinerary of another long stay in Ireland, it would be focused on the island's south-western region. The small harbor towns there were charming. In County Cork, there is actually a water buffalo farm, the first I had heard of, called Toons Bridge Dairy.

The Buffalo in this herd are of the Asian Water Buffalo lineage. They look very similar to cows but with different horns. The owner told me of several advantages to raising water buffalo. They are healthier and heartier than typical cattle. The longer lifespans and lower veterinary bills are a major plus, but the big draw is the milk they produce. It has a whiter look, heavy protein content and makes a very tasty form of mozzarella cheese.

The farm has such a demand for their mozzarella, they rarely have enough milk left to make other cheeses.

The water buffalo are incredibly smart as well. The owner of the herd told us that the buffalo picked up on how the gate latch worked. Using their horns, they were able to open the gate and run for it.

Except they had no interest in running.

They were easily corralled and brought back inside the fences. The latches were changed to prevent further escapes, but the buffalo figured that one out as well. It is easy to make wisecracks about the dangerous animals in Australia, but who knew water buffalo were

PEANUT BUTTER AND PASSPORTS

so crafty? These huge animals may be smarter than some people I know.

Over time, they may figure out how to work in concert—one buffalo creates a diversion, while another picks the pocket of a guest.

The herd may send out the cutest baby in the herd to be fawned over by farm visitors while the edgy buffalo in the herd make off with visitors' vehicles.

The young buffalo have a mat of fur atop their heads that looks like black human hair. For a bald guy like me, it isn't easy to accept that water buffalo have more hair than I do. The youngest males were all sequestered in a barn apart from the rest of the herd. Cute and approachable, they hung out in small pens in duos or trios. It was easy to scratch their heads, though some were licking your hand before you got to their heads. It occurred to me late in the tour that those animals were most likely apart from the rest because they were about to be slaughtered as a source of veal.

Young males from all herds of cattle are raised to live short lives and be a human delicacy. I hate that, but it's been the case for millennia. I have eaten plenty of meat, though less every year, so my protests are a full-out hypocrisy. Yet, I felt like we should try to bust these young fellas out. They could make their way to the surfing beaches and watch the world championships or maybe run for public office with those IQs.

I then realized the situation was under control. The adult buffalo that mastered the latches likely already had a plan to spring these imprisoned young buffalo. Irish police may end up investigating buffalo theft, searching high and low for the human culprits while the adult buffalo in the herd innocently look on, snickering at the less intelligent humans.

EPILOGUE

How does one come up with the book title <u>Peanut Butter and Passports</u>? I chose that name for the podcast months ago because peanut butter is one of my favorite things, and so is my passport. Pretty simple I suppose, but I am a simple guy. Peanut butter represents the simplest, easiest thing to look forward to every day, while passports conjure the expectations of a remarkably memorable trip. Together, they symbolically represent the wide range of good things to look forward to in life.

Recently, I took a poll on the Facebook page of the Peanut Butter and Passports podcast. The question was, "If you were to receive a free trip for Christmas, what destination would you choose?" Those polled were largely from the U.S. The overwhelming winning destination was Italy.

One of the stalwarts of the "old country," Italy has mesmerized travelers for centuries. The country has it all, ranging from the majestic Alps, to the Amalfi coast,

Lake Como and Tuscany. It also has all of the historic cities, well-represented in world history books for good reason.

When discussing travel, you stumble upon many questions without a single correct answer. When I am talking about people's travels, the focus typically centers on food or incredible things to see. To try and compile a list of amazing natural wonders would result in dozens of nominees to consider.

I have tramped the Andes and Rockies and ended each hike shaking my head at the rampant, awe-inspiring landscapes we are fortunate to have been gifted with. I have seen beaches and coasts in too many places to count and can sit entranced for hours enjoying the rhythm of the tides. A shaded balcony overlooking the sea truly does it for me.

The sight and sound of oceans may be the strongest combination to stir human reaction, until the arrival of peanut butter and jelly of course.

Yet those are very general. Choosing "mountains or beach" doesn't whittle down to specific places. If I awarded trophies based on my travels to date, here would be the recipients.

EPILOGUE

Category #1 – Favorite Country Visited

The Nominees

> Cuba
> Peru
> Bolivia
> Canada
> New Zealand
> Ireland
> Mexico

And the winner is . . .

> New Zealand

Category #2 – Most Awe-Inspiring Natural Setting

The Nominees

> Queenstown, New Zealand
> The Cliffs of Moher, Ireland
> Lake Louise, Alberta, Canada
> Milford and Doubtful Sound, New Zealand

The winner is . . .

> Milford and Doubtful Sound, New Zealand

Category #3 – Favorite Town Visited

The Nominees

> Cusco, Peru
> Kinsale, Ireland
> Banff, Alberta, Canada
> Queenstown, New Zealand

The winner is . . .

> Queenstown, New Zealand

A definite pattern was revealed. I feel like I am just starting as a traveler, so things can change, but New Zealand is the Jewel of Earth in my opinion. To many, Tuscany can never be beat. Others love Paris. National parks may be your thing, or possibly being stalked by an anaconda while traversing the Amazon sounds exciting. Those are all correct answers for someone, which is the beauty of traveling.

Sometimes the luckiest people seem to be the ones who drive endlessly "picking" trinkets to be refurbished, resold or repurposed. Long slow days on the road seem mighty nice when your daily norm is a list of things to squeeze in before you go to sleep, knowing you'll have to do it again the next day.

And the next.

EPILOGUE

Sitting on a ranch in Montana oscillates between phenomenal and "please save me," depending upon your views. I know people that dream of "unplugging" and others who hyperventilate when Wi-Fi doesn't work.

One thing I believe to be universally true is how we will look back on our lives during our last day. When your body begins to fail you and your time is short, do you really think having *another* closet full of clothes will seem important when weighed against an additional trip that the money spent on said clothes could have bought you?

A house larger than you need can be a good investment, but buying a smaller one frees up money and time to take a road trip across the U.S., see the Northern Lights, or witness the World's Largest Hells Angel.

People are quick to say, "Life is too short." A short life should be enjoyed, right? For some, that means smoking cigarettes makes sense, while for others it's "pass the cheesecake!" Then there are the health fanatics, trying to squeeze every possible bit of life out of their bodies before their tombstone is installed.

Most end up headed toward careers lasting decades, working far longer than they prefer as prisoners to a broken health insurance system, run by those making money off of it.

Meanwhile, thousands of people from all over the world move to places like Costa Rica, Ecuador, Portugal, Spain and Malaysia and find far better amenities than they imagined. They secure high quality medical coverage for a tiny fraction of the cost and an exciting lifestyle amongst both locals and fellow expats.

On the trips recounted here, both meeting strangers and having time alone to myself helped dull the sadness of the failed romance, a visitor that had *l-o-n-g* overstayed its welcome. The experiences helped me pull the parachute on a teaching career—one I loved but that had grown stale.

Someday I will visit the safari regions of Africa, drive about in Iceland, throw tomatoes at people in Spain (don't worry, it's a tomato-throwing festival) and take other jaunts, just as you may find the love of your life, an unforgettable place, the courage to move or something to simply "foam" over.

Yes, traveling has its hassles, but daily life has more, or we wouldn't want vacations in the first place.

I spoke at my final banquet as a high school head coach, after 36 seasons. I highlighted four quotes and what each of them meant to me and the lesson each held for the athletes listening. One of them applies to all of us and comes from a person with so many physical hardships we should all emulate her positivity.

"Life is either a grand adventure, or nothing at all!"
−Helen Keller

Schedule time for yourself, or for things you *want* to do. Don't fall into routines where you spend a lot of time doing something only *mildly* interesting at best. Be smart with your money so you can take long weekend road trips or vacations frequently.

The quote, "You are the author of your own life story" has become somewhat cliché, yet is mostly true. Each day of your life is like a page in your book, so how do you want your story to end?

The people-watchers are counting on each of us to make it interesting.

ACKNOWLEDGEMENTS

I would like to thank my editors, Lisa Wasmer for tolerating the inanities of what I write and devoting so much time, and Dave Lauer scrubbed my final version masterfully. I enjoyed the process working with you. The manufacturers of red ink pens certainly saw a spike in sales in the weeks leading up to the publishing date.

Thanks as well to Christine Debrecht, Kim Dailey, Kim Reeder and Lacey Miller for conceptual ideas.

The idea of the book stemmed from a simple place. If I enjoy talking about, and hearing of, travel tales how can I do it on a broader scale, with more friends so to speak. The Peanut Butter and Passports podcast was one way of doing that. This book, and future ones, will do that as well. I hope readers feel a little more inspired to take the next trip and are more in tune with the strange fun that walks right by sometimes.

I owe a big thanks to the members of my launch team too. Helping the book get thrust into notice will always be appreciated.

Ebook and paperback formatting by Jen Henderson. Cover design by Ilian Georgiev.

Edited by Lisa Wasmer and Dave Lauer. Some photos from dreamtimeimages.com.

If you enjoy <u>Peanut Butter and Passports</u> please leave a review on Amazon.

ABOUT THE AUTHOR

Tom Gose taught history for 25 years. He also was honored to have coached seemingly everything, serving as a high school head coach of three different sports that totaled 36 seasons. During his final three semesters, the classroom started feeling like a cubicle with windows. He envied every car that drove by and knew that, when one envies a stranger running errands, a change is needed. He loved the students, the rapport and fun, but realizing the sand was running out of his hour glass, Tom took early retirement and made the jump to traveling, writing, podcasting and speaking.

Tom is a "people-person" but likes animals even more. Many future books are planned, including one in which all proceeds for that book will go to animal charities.

As my "Thank You" for buying Peanut Butter and Passports I would love to send you the FREE audio book version. I plan to narrate the book. Please visit the URL below and I will send you the audio book when it is produced.

https://tomgose.com/books/

94457983R00162

Made in the USA
Lexington, KY
29 July 2018